PRAISE FOR *ARMORBEARERS*

MW00396125

In a day of high stress levels and daily tensions, the key word is *relationships, relationships, relationships*. Recognizing this need, Pastor Bryan Cutshall makes a compelling case for the role of an armorbearer as an irreplaceable gift—someone to stand in the gap and help his pastor maintain the delicate balance between confidence in personal abilities and the need to trust God for insight and strength to deal with weakness. As a minister of fifty-four years, forty-two of which I have served as a pastor, I wholeheartedly recommend *Armorbearers* as a book that not only focuses on the problem but also provides a strategic plan of action born from the combination of research and experience.

—*Paul L. Walker, Ph.D.*

Bryan Cutshall has cut to the heart of the need for pastoral support. Having served as a pastor for more than twenty years, I greatly valued those in the church who prayed for me regularly, encouraged me often, and provided emotional support during times of crisis or discouragement. *Armorbearers* gives a practical, biblical description of the role of the armorbearer. I recommend it to you heartily.

—*Raymond F. Culpepper*

Armorbearers speaks to a real need in our church today. Pastors are under attack almost daily and need the strength and support armorbearers can give. Bryan Cutshall, writing from a pastor's perspective, has experienced firsthand the value of having those in the church who prayed for him, supported him, and encouraged him. This book is a must-read for church leaders, pastors, and anyone called to provide support to those in leadership positions.

—*Orville Hagan*

Armorbearers is right on time, a must-read not just for pastors but for laity, as well. It will help clarify the calling and help identify the ones who have been called. Bryan Cutshall has firsthand knowledge of the importance of an armorbearer and writes from this same perspective.

—*Tim Hill*

I believe the key to the local church is the pastor. *Armorbearers* is an excellent resource for helping both pastors and congregations understand the need for this crucial role. Identifying and utilizing those whom God has called to give prayer and emotional support to church leaders is crucial to the success and even survival of the modern-day church leader.

—*Dennis McGuire*

ARMOR BEARERS

ARMOR BEARERS

BRYAN CUTSHALL

WHITAKER
HOUSE

ARMORBEARERS:
Strength and Support for the Spiritual Leader

Bryan Cutshall Ministries
10575 Tesson Ferry Rd.
St. Louis, MO 63123
www.churchtrainer.com

ISBN: 978-1-60374-107-1
eBook ISBN: 978-1-60374-741-7
Printed in the United States of America
© 2005, 2013 by Bryan Cutshall

Whitaker House
1030 Hunt Valley Circle
New Kensington, PA 15068
www.whitakerhouse.com

Library of Congress Cataloging-in-Publication Data (pending)

1 2 3 4 5 6 7 8 9 10 11 **UJ** 20 19 18 17 16 15 14 13

Dedicated to the
staff, elders, and armorbearers
of
Twin Rivers Worship Center,
St. Louis, Missouri.

CONTENTS

Foreword 11

Introduction 13

1. The Choir of Cave Singers 17

2. Empty Pulpits 26

3. What Is an Armorbearer? 36

4. Unsung Heroes 46

5. Who Will Be the One? 56

6. Rites of Passage 66

7. The Ministry of Encouragement 73

8. Armorbearers or Entourages? 80

9. Discerning the Heart of the Moment 88

10. Keepers of the Flame 94

11. Hands On, Hands Up, and Hands Under 104

12. Portraits of Armorbearers 112

The Armorbearer's Pledge 119

About the Author 121

FOREWORD

In this book, Bryan Cutshall has clearly demonstrated his understanding of the struggles, needs, and enemies of the modern-day pastor or church leader. Bryan does a masterful job of clearly and adequately defining the often overlooked and seldom appreciated role of the armorbearer to the pastor or leader. Using biblical examples and ample scriptural references, he paints an accurate portrait of the armorbearer's role, position, and relationship with his or her leader.

He begins by laying the foundation for the need for armorbearers. Writing from personal experience and also using the stories of others, Cutshall describes the challenges and battles that leaders must face, and the need for someone to protect them from attacks and provide support and encouragement. Then, he articulates the biblical description of an armorbearer and gives examples from the Bible, church history, and his personal experience as senior pastor at Twin Rivers Worship Center in St. Louis, Missouri. One of the most powerful chapters of the book deals with the difference between a leader's *armorbearers* and an *entourage*. Bryan includes a tribute to the armorbearers at his church and the Armorbearer's Pledge they use.

Having served in the role of administrative liaison to the general overseer of the Church of God for more than a decade, I found myself readily

11

identifying with the characteristics and principles that Bryan delineates for the armorbearer. He opened my eyes to a new understanding of some of the challenges I have personally faced as I have transitioned through administrations and dealt with the issues of supporting the agenda of a new leader.

I wholeheartedly recommend this book for pastors and laypersons, leaders and their subordinates, and anyone interested in cultivating this ministry of helps.

—Dr. Kenneth R. Bell

INTRODUCTION

I believe in this book. This is why! One day, my phone rang, and before I could make out the voice on the other end, I could feel his pain. He was so desperate for help that all he could say was, "I really don't want to quit, but I don't know what else to do—my life is too toxic." I still didn't know who was on the other end of the line, but I recognized the voice of brokenness, a sound I had heard too many times before. After he "bled out" for a while, his story began to make more sense. He told me of his plans to leave his wife and family, to leave his church, and to start a new life for himself. He pastored a large, successful church, but the pressure had become too great for him. His people loved him and his family but had become too dependent on them. He was trying to be so many things to so many people that he had lost himself in the process. His self-esteem had bottomed out, and it was all he could do to muster courage to make one last phone call pleading for help.

Since he lived almost one thousand miles away, I couldn't meet him in person for a cup of coffee and a supportive embrace. So, I asked him if I could send him some of my early copies of *Armorbearers*. And I gave him the following instructions:

I told him to find ten people who loved his church and were faithful to God, give them each a copy of the book, and ask them to read it in one week.

Next, ask them to gather and discuss the book, without him being present. I knew that if he was there, they wouldn't open up.

I sent the books overnight, and he distributed them. A few days later, the group met, and the Lord "chaired" the meeting. The participants felt convicted that they had allowed their pastor to carry more burdens that he could possibly bear without someone pouring back into him. It was no wonder he was feeling empty and defeated.

A few days later, this pastor called me again, and he said, "Bryan, you are never going to guess what happened!" He told me a story that I will never forget. This group of people who had met to discuss *Armorbearers* had begun to weep in the presence of the Lord. They had gotten in their cars and, as a group, driven to the pastor's house. When he'd opened the door, they'd greeted him, weeping and apologizing. One of them went to his kitchen and brought back a pan of water. They asked him to sit in his living room recliner while, one by one, they took turns washing his feet and praying blessings over his life. Before it was over, his family came into the room, and they all began weeping and praying together.

The good news is that this man still pastors the same church today. He and his wife are happily married, his children have gone into the ministry, and his church is healthy and growing.

As I look across this world and see burned-out pastors and church leaders, the first question that comes to my mind is: "Where are the armorbearers?"

—*Bryan Cutshall*

"David therefore departed from there and escaped to the cave of Adullam. And when his brothers and all his father's house heard it, they went down there to him. And everyone who was in distress, everyone who was in debt, and everyone who was discontented gathered to him. So he became captain over them. And there were about four hundred men with him."
—1 Samuel 22:1–2

1

THE CHOIR
OF CAVE SINGERS

Have you ever just wanted to run away but didn't know where to go? A pastor showed up at my office one day and said, "I just wanted to run away, but I didn't know where to go." I didn't really know him, although I had met him a couple of times while speaking at a conference in his state. I asked, "Why here?" He replied, "I heard you preach a sermon years ago about a stricken shepherd, and all I could think to do was get to the man who preached that sermon, in hopes that he would know what I needed to do."

I used this sermon illustration in a message I preached many years ago. As I got up to preach, all you could see was my nice suit and tie. Early on in the sermon, I took off my coat and vest to reveal that I was wearing a bloody shirt. I had hidden my pain under nice clothing and learned phrases. I titled the sermon "Stricken Shepherds and Scattered Sheep," using the text of Zechariah 13:7: "*Strike the Shepherd, and the sheep will be scattered.*" This biblical principle states that striking a shepherd always results in sheep scattering. When there is pain in a church, we have to find a better way to deal with it than striking the shepherd. I have watched too many bleeding shepherds disguise their pain with vesture and gesture.

17

Hiding Places

Can you image how David felt hiding in that cave? Saul had been throwing spears at him and plotting to kill him. In the midst of this attack, David learned there were many other desperate people in the world besides him. It must have been a large cave to house 400 men and their families who had fled there for refuge.

It is interesting to read about the exploits of David and his band of "merry men," who were still capable of winning battles even though they were ruined financially, steeped in depression, and overwhelmed.

When you run to the cave, remember that, even in your distress, you can still be productive. Just because one or two areas of your life shut down doesn't mean you no longer have a place or purpose. Even the weary need a leader, and God sometimes uses one who has been broken and poured out to lead a group of people who are worn out but still going.

David's band of mighty men is a portrait of many churches. Some of these churches seem to be gathering places for the weary and worn. God often appoints a leader over them who is a skilled "spear dodger."

You don't have to be perfect to do the will of the Lord. As a matter of fact, we are all in the process of becoming what God wants us to be. Some go to the classroom to be perfected, while others go to the blacksmith's shop to be forged in the fires of adversity. But, whether God decides to use knowledge as power or turn pain into power, the end result is still a strong leader who understands how to move people and get things done. I am convinced that the diploma from the school of "hard knocks" is just as valid as the one from the most prestigious institution of learning.

Singing Cave Songs

Some of the most beautiful worship in the world comes from those who are desperate for God.

+ The woman with the issue of blood touched the hem of Jesus' garment and was instantly healed. (See Matthew 9:20–22; Mark 5:25–34; Luke 8:43–48.)

- The woman with the alabaster box changed the atmosphere in a room because of her uninhibited, self-sacrificing praise. (See Matthew 26:6–13.)

- Habakkuk's song is one of the most beautiful expressions of faith ever written, yet it came to him in a time of crisis. (See Habakkuk 3.)

- Paul and Silas sang a song in jail that was so powerful, God miraculously set every prisoner free and saved the jailer and his family, all because two worn-out, broken-down preachers still had a song in the midst of their crisis. (See Acts 16:16–33.)

After forty years of desert living—burying three generations of loved ones, losing Moses, and living by faith—Joshua finally arrived at Jericho, the first city to be conquered in the Canaan land. Joshua tried to rally his bedraggled troops to battle; indeed, they were ready to go with him. But when they stood on the edge of their first battlefield, Joshua asked the angel, "What are our battle instructions?" The angel must have smiled as he said to Joshua, "God wants you to march around the city seven days, and then, on the seventh day, He wants you to shout." (See Joshua 5:13–6:5.) Joshua must have wondered, *After all I have been through, can I still show up with a shout?*

Worship from hurting, broken, and desperate people gets God's attention. Matthew 15 tells the story of a woman who cried out to get Jesus' attention. Her demon-possessed daughter needed His help. After several failed attempts at crying out to Jesus, she changed her method of approach. She decided to approach Him through worship. As she began to worship, He turned to her and spoke the words that freed her daughter from the demon that ruled her life. God loves "cave songs."

David wrote some of his most beautiful music from that cave. One of the continuing themes of David's songs is *"out of the depth."* He used this phrase many times to describe the estate of his existence. He also used the word *refuge* over and over to describe God as his hiding place.

Listen to the words of one of David's songs and see if you can picture a young man with his harp singing beside a campfire in the cave of refuge:

> *Have mercy on me, O LORD, for I am in trouble;*
> *My eye wastes away with grief,*
> *Yes, my soul and my body!*

For my life is spent with grief,
And my years with sighing;
My strength fails because of my iniquity,
And my bones waste away.
I am a reproach among all my enemies,
But especially among my neighbors,
And am repulsive to my acquaintances;
Those who see me outside flee from me.
I am forgotten like a dead man, out of mind;
I am like a broken vessel.
For I hear the slander of many;
Fear is on every side;
While they take counsel together against me,
They scheme to take away my life.

But as for me, I trust in You, O Lord;
I say, "You are my God."
My times are in Your hand;
Deliver me from the hand of my enemies,
And from those who persecute me....

You shall hide them in the secret place of Your presence
From the plots of man;
You shall keep them secretly in a pavilion
From the strife of tongues....

Be of good courage,
And He shall strengthen your heart,
All you who hope in the Lord.

—Psalm 31:9–15, 20, 24

The Choir of Cave Singers

Many people who are reading this book belong to the choir of cave singers. Your paths have not been easy. But, in the midst of your despair, remember that God loves cave songs. Don't forget to sing. There is no way to hear the choir on this side of heaven, for the members are scattered throughout all the earth. However, God hears their song. As each voice is raised toward heaven, it joins in a massive chorus that reaches the ears of the Almighty. Who is in this choir, you ask? Their names will not be mentioned, but here is a description of their song:

Verse 1

God hears the cries of...

> those who have preached to cold or empty pews.
> those who never got an "Amen."
> those who have propped themselves up to preach.
> those who beat out the paths so others could find their way.
> those who logged midnight hours.

Verse 2

God shows mercy to...

> those who had to hold back their own tears so that someone
>   else could cry.
> ✗ those who have given more care than they ever received.
> those who fill others' hands but walk away empty-handed.
> those who watched others take the credit for their hard work
>   and never said a word.
> those who bled so that others could belong.

Verse 3

God gives blessings to...

> those who never owned a house.
> those who never saw the ocean.
> those who were limited by the traditions of men.
> those who dreamed in silence.
> those whose courage outmatched their fears.

Verse 4

God answered the prayers of...

those who lifted up weary hands.
those who trimmed their own wicks and kept their own flame.
those who turned paths into trails and trails into roads.
those who had to cross the finish line limping.
those who showed up, never gave up, and are one day going up
for saying yes to God.

Just like Jacob, you were transformed when you were left alone. Like Elijah, you pressed on in spite of fear and depression. Like Noah, you preached on, even when your message was rejected. Like Paul, you have mastered midnight praise. Like Jonah, you allowed your misfortune to serve as a lesson for other people's fortune. Like David, you sang your best songs in a cave.

You prayed hard, you loved hard, you cared hard; you gave again, you sang again, you preached again, you danced again; you dared to dream dreams, you flew the flag, and you smiled despite your adversities.

You are the choir of cave singers.

I vividly recall where I was when I wrote the first draft of this chapter. I had gone away for several days of solitude, prayer, and writing. As I wrote each line of the "Cave Song," I could identify a name and a face with each phrase. I sat at a small table in a cabin by a river and wept for all the ministers I was writing about; I could feel their desperation in each line. What can be read in mere minutes took me hours to write, because I stopped after each line and prayed for a pastor. When I finished, I sat in silence and held my breath. We have many prominent pastors in our country who have earned their places in the spotlight of success. We need to learn from them, but they, too, have paid a high price. No one will ever know the true cost of their toil.

Let us never forget the faithful soldiers who bleed on the Christian battlefield each day. Their names may never be recorded in the annals of human history, yet they are more famous in heaven than most renowned men on earth. One day, angels will line up to shake the hands of heaven's heroes.

DISCUSSION POINTS

1. Worship from hurting, broken, and desperate people gets God's attention. Are you a cave singer? What is your song?

2. Discuss the text of 1 Samuel 22:1–2.

3. Read and then discuss the lyrics of Habakkuk's song in Habakkuk 3.

4. What psalm of David could be your cave song?

5. Pick out two or three types of people in the choir of cave singers and discuss the types of situations God may use to turn their pain into power.

6. How can you be productive in the midst of adversity?

"Then [Jesus] said to His disciples, 'The harvest truly is plentiful, but the laborers are few. Therefore pray the Lord of the harvest to send out laborers into His harvest.'"
—Matthew 9:37–38

2

EMPTY PULPITS

The harvest has never been the problem. There have always been plenty of sinners to fill each empty seat in every church. While we need to be concerned with the problem of empty pews, we have another emerging crisis on our hands that will have an even more devastating effect on God's church. It's not an empty pew but an empty pulpit. If there are no ministers, even those occupying the pews will eventually leave.

The statistics are staggering:

- 13 percent of active pastors are divorced.

- 23 percent of pastors have been fired or pressured to resign at least once in their careers.

- 25 percent of pastors don't know where to turn when they have a family or personal conflict.

- 25 percent of pastors' wives see their husband's work schedule as a source of conflict.

- 40 percent of pastors—and 47 percent of their spouses—are suffering from burnout, frantic schedules, and/or unrealistic expectations.

- 45 percent of pastors say that they've experienced depression or burnout to the extent that they needed to take a leave of absence.

- 50 percent of pastors feel unable to meet the demands of their job.

- 52 percent of pastors and their spouses believe that being in pastoral ministry is hazardous to their family's health and well-being.

- 70 percent of pastors have no close friends.

- 56 percent of pastors' wives have no close friends.

- 57 percent of pastors say that they would leave the pastorate if they had somewhere else to go or another vocation they could do.

- 75 percent of pastors report having suffered from severe stress that caused anguish, worry, bewilderment, anger, depression, fear, and alienation.

- 80 percent of pastors say they have insufficient time to spend with their spouse.

- 80 percent of pastors believe that pastoral ministry has had negative effects on their family.

- 90 percent of pastors feel unqualified or poorly prepared for ministry.

- 94 percent of pastors feel under pressure to have a perfect family.

- 1,500 pastors leave their ministries each month due to burnout, conflict, or moral failure.

- Doctors, lawyers, and clergy exhibit the highest levels of drug abuse, alcoholism, and suicide than any other profession.[1]

According to the Francis Schaeffer Institute of Church Leadership Survey:

- 90 percent of pastors report working between 55 to 75 hours per week.

- 70 percent of pastors feel grossly underpaid.

- Only 1 out of 10 ministers will actually be able to retire.

- 4,000 new churches are planted each year, and 7,000 churches close.

- More than 1,700 pastors left the ministry every month during 2011.

- During that same year, more than 1,300 pastors per month were terminated by their churches, many without cause.

---

1. http://www.pastorburnout.com/pastor-burnout-statistics.html.

+ 50 percent of pastors are so discouraged that they would leave the ministry if they could, but have no other way of making a living.[2]

And according to George Barna Research:

+ 33 percent of pastors leave church due to conflict with the congregation.

✗ + The average tenure of associate ministers and staff is less than two years.

+ An estimated 25 percent of all pastors relocate every year.

+ According to John Maxwell, most conflict in the church that causes a pastor to leave is due to fewer than eight people, regardless of the size of the church.

+ Clergy divorce has risen 65 percent in the last twenty years.

+ 71 percent of pastors say they're having financial problems.

Jane Rubietta, a pastor's wife and author of *How to Keep the Pastor You Love*, writes, "After a few years in ministry, I saw so many casualties across the country—broken pastors, church conflict, abandoned callings, too-brief stays at churches, and burnout—that I virtually called every denomination head in the mid-90s and asked, 'What are you doing for your pastors?'"

She goes on to say, "Caring for pastors goes beyond gifts and treats. If the pastor loses his love for God, he will certainly lose his ability to lead the church." In her book, she breaks down the largely unexamined myth of the superhuman pastor.[3]

Occupied Pulpits but with Empty Words

Job 21:34 says, *"How then can you comfort me with empty words, since falsehood remains in your answers?"* Long before the pulpit is vacant, the heart of the minister is vacant. Forced to rely on the relics of "preacher jargon" and clichés, the minister steps into his comfort zone each week to spread on another thin layer of the gospel. Empty words reveal an empty soul. Jesus said that from the abundance of the heart, the mouth speaks. (See Matthew 12:34; Luke 6:45.) The same is true about the lack of abundance. From the emptiness of the heart, the mouth also speaks.

2. http://www.pastoralcareinc.com/statistics/.

3. For more information on Jane Rubietta and her book, visit www.abounding.org.

Warmed-over sermons with new titles reflect a loss of passion. Too many ministers are in the habit of preaching sermons instead of giving a message. There is a difference. A sermon consists of just enough of the gospel to make it legitimate, just enough illustrations to make it interesting, and just enough of an outline to make it readable. A message, on the other hand, starts with "knee-ology," flows through theology, and comes out hot, spicy, and full of flavor. Sermons stir only the emotions, while messages change lives with timely, relevant, convicting, fresh-baked daily bread.

There are many things God wants to accomplish that cannot be achieved through a sermon. There are times when only a "word from the Lord" will get the job done. There are too many ministers and congregations who are hungry for a word from the Lord—a timely, fitly spoken, well-ordered word that loosens the bands and breaks the yokes that are holding back our lives and mission.

Job 21:34 indicates that *"empty words"* cannot and will not comfort, for they are underlain with falsehood. This does not mean that they are necessarily a blatant or premeditated lie; rather, they are spoken from an attitude of insincerity. If you don't truly believe it, you can't really sell it.

Often, the congregants are already spiritually starving before they leave a church. Many of the sheep—even faithful ones—die a little each week from spiritual malnutrition. They try to live on the dry, old morsels of stale spiritual food or on food too diluted to sustain them. The weakened shepherd no longer has the passion to properly prepare the spiritual table. Even those who live on spiritual bread and water often fall in the heat of the battle. Warriors must eat well in order to bring home the spoils of victory.

Exit Interviews

This section features interviews with several pastors who have walked away from the ministry. While their stories have been printed by permission, their names have been changed to protect their families from further turmoil.

Interview #1—George

George is a college graduate with degrees in theology and psychology. All through college, he and his young bride dreamed of pastoring their first church together. She worked so that he could attend college full-time. Meanwhile, they had two children who were content to live in their small apartment, furnished sparsely with the bare essentials—books, paper, and a computer. Life was focused: education now, ministry later.

Soon after George graduated, he was appointed to a church of about 150 people in the suburbs of a large city. This was a dream come true. Drawing from all of his educational experience, he began to build what he thought was a great game plan. It wasn't long before George ran into a roadblock called "tradition." The congregation was comfortable with how things were. They simply wanted George to do what each of their previous pastors had done—maintain.

George's lack of experience began to show in how he dealt with the people. When he assumed his fighting stance, the battle of tradition versus pastoral authority was on. Soon, a petition for his resignation surfaced. A secret meeting was called, and George was voted out by an overwhelming majority. With their hopes dashed and dreams shattered, George and his young family decided that perhaps the ministry was not the place for them, after all. This disillusioned couple began to struggle financially, and their marriage began to be filled with turmoil; it ultimately ended in divorce.

Today, George is remarried to an unbeliever and doesn't attend church. This came about three years after he lost his job and about two years after his divorce was finalized. His ex-wife and their children have found refuge in a church of a different denomination. They are still struggling, financially and emotionally.

I often wonder if George's ministry and family could have been saved if someone from an older generation would have been available to speak wisdom into his life. Armorbearers are not fellow pastors teaching us "how to do ministry." They are usually laymen who support and encourage a minister as they grow into their calling.

Where were the armorbearers?

Interview #2—Tim and Jan

Tim and Jan appeared to be the perfect couple cut out for ministry. He was as enthusiastic as a man could be about serving God, and his zeal and passion made him the obvious choice for a staff role in a medium-sized church. At first, it seemed like a match made in heaven. The senior pastor was happy with the work of Tim and Jan, and the church loved them both dearly.

After a few months, the warm reception and wide influence of young Tim started to make the senior pastor feel somewhat insecure. Soon, he began questioning Tim's motives and decisions. The dagger was buried, and the bleeding started. The wounds just got deeper and more infected as time passed. Piercing words of accusation, and resulting feelings of pain, became the norm.

After contacting a few people in their denomination's leadership, Tim and Jan soon learned that everyone was siding with the senior pastor. Lack of tenure, experience, and relationships placed them at the mercy of a time-honored system of politics and power. Their zeal and innocence proved to be no match for such a formidable opponent. In the end, they were left without an ally, representative, or advocate. Their options were depleted, along with their security and support.

Deeply wounded, they decided to leave the ministry altogether, for fear of another breach of trust such as they had undergone. Tim's lament was the same as David's: "No man cared for my soul."

Where were the armorbearers?

Interview #3—Pastor Bob

Pastor Bob was a seasoned man of fifty-seven years. He had overseen the construction of many buildings and had proven to be a choice administrator and church builder. His track record was clean and concise. He was appointed to a new congregation, following in the steps of a long-term minister who had decided to stay at the church and be involved as a layperson. The first couple of years seemed to go well.

After the new board was elected, one of the board members, a relative of the former pastor, had a disagreement with Pastor Bob. One thing led to another, and soon, the church was up in arms, with the former pastor leading the band against Pastor Bob. The event came to a head at a conference where Pastor Bob stood as the target, while one person after another took potshots at him.

One exaggerated story after another surfaced, until his good name was marred with false accusations, his character defamed. The disheartened seasoned warrior did not have the strength to start over, and so he slipped off quietly into the shadows. His early retirement and broken heart led him to an early grave.

Where were the armorbearers?

Interview #4—Gary and Charlotte

Gary and Charlotte left Bible school filled with ambition. Like most other young couples going into ministry, they were going to change the world with their songs and words. With his new blue suit, and with her beautiful dress and never-ending charm, they set out on their assignment. As in many small churches, they were viewed more as "caretakers" rather than a couple God had sent to lead the congregation to higher ground.

At first, things were fine. Their youthful zeal and desire to please God were enough to meet the demands placed on them. Charlotte didn't mind cleaning the church building, and Gary didn't mind mowing the lawn, painting the walls, and doing other handy chores. But soon, one demand turned into two, and two multiplied into four. In their willingness to work, it wasn't long before they were enabling the people they served to do nothing. The whole load fell on Gary and Charlotte. Burdened down, they began to feel worn out, tired, and a bit resentful. They were the ones who prayed, visited, labored, and cared for the sick, the depressed, the dying, and the lonely. They served everyone else—including those who didn't even attend their church.

In a few months, they felt the stress taking a toll on their marriage, their attitudes, and their health. No longer did they have time for each other and the plans they wanted to make. It took them about three years in those trenches to decide that the ministry was not for them. With their hopes and dreams dashed, this young couple left the church feeling burned out and mistreated.

This story did not have to end this way. First, Gary and Charlotte did not have enough training or experience to know that you must raise up leaders and delegate responsibilities to them.

Second, no one in that congregation felt the calling to be an armorbearer. A single armorbearer could have saved their ministry. Gary and Charlotte both have good jobs today and are still married and serving the Lord; however, the kingdom of God will never know the harvest that was assigned to their lives, and the potential for success they could have had, all because there was no armorbearer serving them.

Pastor Wayne Cordeiro, of New Hope Christian Fellowship in Oahu, Hawaii, wrote a life-changing book for leaders called *Leading on Empty*. It is filled with great strategies on how to keep from living an empty life. After reading this book, I started two practices in my life that I think are game changers. First, I listen to at least two sermons by other ministers every week. This helps to teach me and to keep me filled up spiritually. Second, I live a life of strategic solitude. In other words, I plan days in my schedule every month to be alone for prayer and meditation. Leading on empty is the prelude to empty pews and empty pulpits.

Read book "Leading on Empty"

DISCUSSION POINTS

1. Read and discuss the Empty Pulpits statistics.

2. What are some ways in which you could encourage your pastor and protect his love for the church? Remember, if the pastor loses his love for God, he certainly will lose his ability to lead the church.

3. Read the four exit interviews again and discuss how the role of an armorbearer would have helped each pastor.

4. Take time to pray for your pastor and the staff of your church.

"Greater love has no one than this, than to lay down one's life for his friends. You are My friends if you do whatever I command you. No longer do I call you servants, for a servant does not know what his master is doing; but I have called you friends, for all things that I heard from My Father I have made known to you."
—John 15:13–15

3

WHAT IS AN ARMORBEARER?

The word *armorbearer* appears eighteen times in the *New King James Version* of the Bible. It comes from two Hebrew words: *nasa* (pronounced "naw-saw"), which means "to lift, bear up, carry," and *keliy* (pronounced "kel-lee"), which means "vessel, implement." Combined, the definition of an *armorbearer* is "a vessel or implement that lifts up and bears up the leader."

In many cases, the assignment cannot be completed because there is no armorbearer. The weary warrior has no other option except to rest and regain his strength while the troops wait on the sidelines for his recovery.

Between the passes, by which Jonathan sought to go over to the Philistines' garrison, there was a sharp rock on one side and a sharp rock on the other side. And the name of one was Bozez, and the name of the other Seneh. The front of one faced northward opposite Michmash, and the other southward opposite Gibeah. Then Jonathan said to the young man who bore his armor, "Come, let us go over to the garrison of these uncircumcised; it may be that the LORD will work for us. For nothing restrains the LORD from saving by many or by few." So his armorbearer said to him, "Do all that is in your heart. *Go then; here I am with you, according to your heart."* Then Jonathan said, "Very well, let us cross over to these men, and we will show ourselves to them. If they say thus to us, 'Wait until we come to you,' then we will stand still in our place and not go up to them. But if they say thus, 'Come up to us,' then we will go up. For the LORD has delivered them into our hand, and this will be a sign to us." So both of them showed themselves to the garrison of the Philistines. And the Philistines said, "Look, the Hebrews are coming out of the holes where they have hidden." Then the men of the garrison called to Jonathan and his armorbearer, and said, "Come up to us, and we will show you something." Jonathan said to his armorbearer, "Come up after me, for the LORD has delivered them into the hand of Israel." And Jonathan climbed up on his hands and knees with his armorbearer after him; and they fell before Jonathan. And as he came after him, his armorbearer killed them. That first slaughter which Jonathan and his armorbearer made was about twenty men within about half an acre of land. And there was trembling in the camp, in the field, and among all the people. The garrison and the raiders also trembled; and the earth quaked, so that it was a very great trembling. Now the watchmen of Saul in Gibeah of Benjamin looked, and there was the multitude, melting away; and they went here and there. Then Saul said to the people who were with him, "Now call the roll and see who has gone from us." And when they had called the roll, surprisingly, Jonathan and his armorbearer were not there.* (1 Samuel 14:4–17)

The Honor of the Armorbearer

The honor of an armorbearer is dependent on one thing only: he must bring his leader back from the battle alive. Imagine a raging battle, and an army in need of true leadership in order to win. The leader is their greatest hope for winning. His experience, wisdom, and training can get them through—if he can get to the battlefield.

On the day of this great battle, there is one who wakes before the leader to begin making preparations. He is the armorbearer. The first duty of his day is to sharpen the sword of the leader. After that, he sharpens his own sword. Next, he shines the armor of his leader. It is important that the leader stand out from the rest of the army so that the soldiers may see him clearly, for they look to him for direction.

After the armor is polished and ready, the armorbearer goes to the stables to bridle the fastest horses he can find to pull their chariot. He hitches the team and pulls up to the quarters of the leader to take him to the battleground. The armorbearer drives the chariot while the leader rests, so that nothing should distract him from focusing on the battle plan. The armorbearer also refreshes the leader with water and food. It is of utmost importance that the leader be ready and strong for the battle.

Upon arriving at the battlefield, the armorbearer stops the chariot and proceeds to help the leader strap on his armor. He hands him his freshly sharpened weapon. Then, he puts on his own armor and takes up his sword. The armorbearer listens for the instructions of the leader and guides the chariot to the strategic location of the command center. The leader has one goal in mind—winning the battle. The armorbearer's goal is to bring his leader back from the battle, alive and unharmed. There will be other battles, and he must preserve the life of the one who can lead the army to victory. The honor of the leader is victory, but the honor of the armorbearer is the life of his leader.

If the enemy overtakes the chariot, the leader will take up arms and begin to fight as a foot soldier. The armorbearer will leave the chariot behind and take his place with the leader. His place is not at the leader's side or in front of him but rather at his back. The leader is a skilled warrior, but he needs someone to watch his back so that the enemy cannot sneak up on him unawares. Wherever the leader goes in battle, the armorbearer fights at his back.

✳ *Traits and Duties of the Armorbearer*

- Strengthens his leader
- Willing to take a risk with his leader
- Instinctively knows his leader's thoughts
- Feels a deep sense of respect for his leader
- Agrees with his leader and submits to his authority and leadership
- Repels any kind of attack against his leader

- Rescues his leader from difficulties and hardships
- Keeps one eye on his leader and the other eye trained on the enemy
- Carries out every plan of his leader
- Watches while his leader sleeps and awakens him whenever a foe attacks
- Cares for his leader's belongings
- Brings acceleration and promotion to his leader's progress
- Reacts with total intolerance to any false accusations against his leader
- Refreshes his leader's journey by personally serving and waiting on him
- Aids his leader in spiritual combat
- Understands his assignment and also the assignment of his leader

Between the Passes

Between the passes, by which Jonathan sought to go over to the Philistines' garrison, there was a sharp rock on one side and a sharp rock on the other side. And the name of one was Bozez, and the name of the other Seneh. The front of one faced northward opposite Michmash, and the other southward opposite Gibeah. (1 Samuel 14:4–5)

It is not by mere coincidence that God lists the names of these two stones. Their names reveal the place where armorbearers are needed the most. *Bozez* means "shining," and *Seneh* means "thorny." Similarly, the Chinese word for "crisis" is made up of two symbols. One symbol is tragedy; the other is opportunity. What a true picture of a crisis. On one side, you have an opportunity; on the other side, you have a tragedy.

It is between "shining" and "thorny" that you need the strength of another. On one hand, you are wonderful; on the other hand, you can't do anything right. Caught in the middle of glistening and thorny, you are pulled between the opinions and labels of other people.

This passageway is analogous to the route every person must travel. The route is made up of successes and failures—moments of glory (shining) and moments of disappointment (thorny). This is the place where you are the most confused about yourself and the most vulnerable to the attacks of the enemy. You struggle to find the balance between knowing your strengths and sensing what you still need to learn. You wrestle with the knowledge you possess and the power to build up; yet, you still seem to have the power to destroy.

You must not allow yourself to see only your strengths (shining), or you will become overly confident in your own abilities. At the same time, you must not become too focused on your weaknesses (thorny), or you will be overcome with fear and low self-esteem. This passage is a good place to be because it is the balance between confidence in your gifts and the need to trust God in your weaknesses. It is the symmetry of reality. No one is good at everything, and only the self-righteous get entangled in the web of self-deceit. It is good to see both your strengths and your weaknesses in order to gather a staff that will compensate for your frailties.

This is where your armorbearer becomes an irreplaceable gift in your life. The armorbearer stands in the gap with you, between glistening and thorny, to keep you balanced. You cannot continue to live off the glory of your last breakthrough before the battle is over. Breakthroughs are not victories. Neither can you live in the shadow of your last defeat, knowing delay is not denial. This vulnerable area is a place of struggle where you must know yourself and keep your life in balance.

The Decision to Fight

Then Jonathan said to the young man who bore his armor, "Come, let us go over to the garrison of these uncircumcised; it may be that the Lord *will work for us. For nothing restrains the* Lord *from saving by many or by few." So his armorbearer said to him, "Do all that is in your heart. Go then; here I am with you, according to your heart."*   (1 Samuel 14:6–7)

Jonathan admits that he does not know for sure what the outcome will be: *"It may be that the* Lord *will work for us."* As an armorbearer, you don't always know if the decision of your leader is the right one. Your commitment to bring your leader back from the battle is crucial at this point. There are times when your leader may use all of the wisdom, knowledge, and experience at his or her disposal to make a tough call, yet he or she still may be wrong. Only one who is truly called to be an armorbearer can stand next to the bloodied leader and bleed alongside him or her. There will be other days for victory; don't lose hope on the "thorny" days.

In 1999, our church decided to relocate. We had been trying to purchase a shopping center, and the arrangements looked promising. To pay for it, we needed to sell our existing building. I was surrounded with wise counsel as we embarked on this risky business. We accepted a contract and a down payment for our building and proceeded with our plans. Within weeks of closing, the deal on the shopping center fell through. I had to stand before my congregation and tell them that we had to give up our facility with no place to go. All I could do was ask them to trust me. We had not acted hastily, but, nevertheless, things were not turning out the way we had planned.

I will never forget the final Sunday in our old church. It was emotional for some, unsettling for all. For the near term, we decided to meet in the gymnasium of a school located about ten miles away. Unforeseen by us, we continued to grow, even without a building. We outgrew that school gymnasium in about three months. Over the next two years, we moved eighteen times before settling into the building we now call home. I do not consider this a defeat at all. We had to stick together and follow God through our "see-nothing" days.

It was my armorbearers who kept me encouraged during this trying time. It would seem natural for someone to wonder whether I had truly heard from the Lord on that business deal. I still believe I acted in the best of wisdom, but I understand that God may have had a different plan. In the end, we added another 300 members during those two years, and God has used the story of our "following the cloud" to encourage thousands of other weary pastors who have found themselves somewhere between the glistening and the thorny places.

Jonathan's armorbearer had to make the decision to stand by his leader, even though there were risks involved. When an armorbearer truly feels called of the Lord to serve his leader, he does not keep his eye on the battle—he keeps his eye on the leader and the enemy.

So his armorbearer said to him, "Do all that is in your heart. Go then; here I am with you, according to your heart." (1 Samuel 14:7)

The armorbearer understood his calling. He said, in essence, "My job is not to question you; it is simply to serve you. God didn't call me to advise you but to keep you alive. I will follow you as you follow God. If we die today, it will be an honorable death. If we live, it will be a great victory."

I've Got Your Back

So both of them showed themselves to the garrison of the Philistines. And the Philistines said, "Look, the Hebrews are coming out of the holes where they have hidden." Then the men of the garrison called to Jonathan and his armorbearer, and said, "Come up to us, and we will show you something." Jonathan said to his armorbearer, "Come up after me, for the LORD has delivered them into the hand of Israel." And Jonathan climbed up on his hands and knees with his armorbearer after him; and they fell before Jonathan. And as he came after him, his armorbearer killed them.

(1 Samuel 14:11–13)

God was going to deliver the Philistine army into the hands of two men. Great risks often bring great victories. Look at the order of this relationship. The leader goes in first, while the armorbearer covers his back. When you are on the same team, and both of you are fulfilling your calling to the Lord, both of you win.

It doesn't matter who goes first, because one will not succeed without the strength of the other. There is a secret to advancing in God's kingdom: You can lead only as well as you can follow. The route to leadership is *followship*, not fellowship. It isn't about position; it's about obedience. Serving your leader is not about being his friend; it's about being his servant. It is your servitude that God will reward, not your fellowship. Many people who want to lead do not want to serve. Many seek a title instead of a task. But God is choosing tomorrow's leaders from today's labor force.

"And as he came after him, his armorbearer killed them." The armorbearer was fighting at the back of his leader, not at his side. Being an armorbearer is not about being a partner or even an assistant. It is about being behind the scenes as a protector. Because of the position of the armorbearer, no one could sneak up behind the leader. Jonathan's armorbearer was saying to the leader, "Stay on the offense, and I will be your defense." He killed only those who came after Jonathan. As they came after the leader, the armorbearer came after them. A leader cannot fight the enemy while looking over his shoulder. It is the strategic position of the armorbearer that allows the leader to fight without looking back.

The Honorable Discharge

In the military, a person leaving his time of service receives either an honorable or a dishonorable discharge. The type of discharge he receives determines the type of retirement benefits he will receive for his years of service. A person who receives an honorable discharge will enjoy those benefits for the rest of his life.

Likewise, armorbearers do not serve for their entire lives. They go through new seasons of life, and, in cases like Joshua, they may even become the next leader. However, they must never dishonor themselves or the honor of their calling by stabbing their leader in the back. Their calling is a heavenly one, but even if they are released from their duty by the Lord, they still have a responsibility to uphold the code of honor. Those who dishonor themselves in service lose their benefits, rank, and reward for their years of service. Armorbearers must remain honorable before the Lord, trusting that, in due time, God will honor them. The bottom line is this: you are either an honorable person or you are not; it has nothing to do with your assignment but everything to do with your character.

DISCUSSION POINTS

1. How can you lift up your pastor until the job is finished?

2. How can you fight and sharpen your pastor's sword?

3. Discuss the duties of an armorbearer. Do you see yourself fulfilling any of them?

4. Do you find yourself in between the "shining" and the "thorns"? Explain why.

5. What are your strengths? What weakness(es) do you have that have required you to trust in God?

6. Remember, your job is not to question your pastor but to serve him or her. Follow your pastor as your pastor follows God. What steps should be taken when we don't understand our pastor?

7. A leader cannot fight the enemy while looking over his shoulder. How can you "have your leader's back"?

8. Discuss the types of behavior that could lead to a "dishonorable discharge."

"Women received their dead raised to life again. And others were tortured, not accepting deliverance, that they might obtain a better resurrection. Still others had trial of mockings and scourgings, yes, and of chains and imprisonment. They were stoned, they were sawn in two, were tempted, were slain with the sword. They wandered about in sheepskins and goatskins, being destitute, afflicted, tormented; of whom the world was not worthy. They wandered in deserts and mountains, in dens and caves of the earth."
—Hebrews 11:35–38

4

UNSUNG HEROES

What is a hero? Technically, a hero is one who is admired for courage or outstanding achievement. Many courageous heroes will never get a parade, a crown, or a seat of honor on this earth. Yet heaven knows their names, and their seat of honor is still waiting for them. The Bible calls them a people *"of whom the world [is] not worthy"* (Hebrews 11:38)

The Armorbearer of Charles Finney

Charles Finney was one of the greatest evangelists who ever lived. He preached in the 1820s and was met with opposition nearly every place he went. Even though people ridiculed him and plotted against him, Finney pushed back the gates of hell in every city he ministered. It seemed as though he was unstoppable. His messages changed entire towns. In fact, mobs tended to greet him because word had spread that when Finney left, the town would be changed. Those who didn't want spiritual revival often met him at the city gates, with threats and promises to keep him out.

What they didn't know was that, about three or four weeks before Finney arrived in a city, a man by the name of Father Daniel Nash would go before him and pray for hours each day over the town. Nash, an Episcopal priest, never attended the revival meetings, staying instead in his hideout praying. Much of the public never discovered the secret to the power behind Finney's preaching. In one town, the best Nash could find was a damp cellar, but this became his center for intercession. Usually, he would try to enlist one or two other people in the town to pray with him. He would train them, and then, when he left, they would continue the prayer covering.

In his journal, Finney wrote,

When I got to town to start the revival, a lady contacted me who ran a boardinghouse. She said, "Brother Finney, do you know a Father Nash? He and two other men have been in my boardinghouse for the last three days, but they haven't eaten a bite of food. I opened the door to peep in on them to see if they were all right and I saw them laying on their faces in a dark room groaning like sick men." She said, "I thought something awful must have happened to them. I was afraid and didn't know what to do. They have been like this for three days. Can you come and check on them?"

Father Nash rarely was seen in public, especially during revival services; but, on one occasion, a gang confronted Finney after a service and threatened him. Finney writes:

Out of a dark shadow steps my good friend Nash. He said to this gang, "Now mark me, young men! God will break your ranks in less than one week, either by converting some of you or sending some of you to hell. He will do this as certainly as He is my God."

By the next Tuesday morning, the leader of the gang had fallen on his knees before Finney and repented of his sins; he then led his gang to the Lord.

In the winter of 1831, Father Nash died. In a cemetery in northern New York State, near the Canadian border, lies the body of Daniel Nash. If you find that old, neglected cemetery, on a cheap tombstone, you will read, "Daniel Nash, Laborer with Finney, Mighty in Prayer, Nov. 17, 1775–Dec. 20, 1831."

Daniel Nash never achieved elite status or notoriety in his time. Most people would have found this humble man unworthy of comment, but Daniel Nash was well-known in heaven—and notorious in hell. Nash did exploits for the King.

Elisha, Armorbearer of the Prophet Elijah

But Jehoshaphat said, "Is there no prophet of the Lord here, that we may inquire of the Lord by him?" So one of the servants of the king of Israel answered and said, "Elisha the son of Shaphat is here, who poured water on the hands of Elijah." (2 Kings 3:11)

How many people would settle for being known as the man *"who poured water on the hands of Elijah"*? When you are the armorbearer, you don't see the leader just when he is calling fire down from heaven; you also see him when he is struggling as a mere man. You see the ordinary side of the one you serve. Elisha was there when Elijah called fire out of heaven (see 2 Kings 1:9–12), but he was also in the cave when Elijah was suffering from depression (see 1 Kings 19:5–18).

He was also on the hillside when King Ahab sent fifty men to bring Elijah in. Elijah was so afraid, he called fire down to kill them. Elisha saw his fear, his vulnerability, his struggle, and his depression. But, after serving him faithfully for almost twenty years, he said, in effect, "Before you go, I want a double portion of what you have. I know you are just a man, but I recognize you as the 'voice of the Lord,' and it has been my privilege to pour water on your hands, cook your meals, carry your scrolls, and refresh you on your journey."

The Bible records several occasions when Elijah tried to leave Elisha behind while he went on a journey, only to have Elisha say, "No. I go where you go. I will not leave your side." We cannot flow in the anointing of Elisha until we first learn to serve an Elijah.

There is only so much you can learn from reading a book or sitting in a classroom. While head knowledge is certainly profitable, it lacks the smells, shadows, tastes, and voices of personal experience. The best preparation is on-the-job training. If God calls you to be an armorbearer, He is offering you the benefits of the struggles, experiences, and victories of another person's entire life. That is a book worth reading. It's not a book of pages and paper but one written on the trails of life. The opportunity to learn from another man's experiences is priceless.

There is no guarantee that an armorbearer is in training for leadership but, many times, this is the very route God uses to bring a person into greatness. Sometimes, God raises up armorbearers to continue the work of their leaders and mentor. Perhaps this experience is necessary to truly know the heart and vision of their assignment from God. The Lord did not raise up one from the house of Elijah to succeed him; He raised up his armorbearer as a successor.

The pattern of God raising up a righteous seed instead of a natural seed is found throughout the Bible. God did not raise up one of Moses' two sons; He raised up Joshua, his armorbearer. In Joshua 1:1, Joshua is called "Moses' minister" (KJV).

God did not raise up Jonathan to be the king after his father Saul, but He raised up Saul's armorbearer, David. (See 1 Samuel 16:14–23.) Even when Saul became jealous of David and sought to kill him, David, the faithful armorbearer, was true to the end. He never raised a hand against his leader, King Saul.

God did not raise up one of Eli's sons as the priest in his place, but He raised up Eli's armorbearer, a boy by the name of Samuel, who became one of the greatest prophets in Israel. (See 1 Samuel 3.) On many occasions, the anointing and success of the armorbearer exceeds that of the one he serves, but it is in his role of the servant that God chooses him, anoints him, and establishes him.

The Reward of the Armorbearer

But Jehoshaphat said, "Is there no prophet of the LORD here, that we may inquire of the LORD by him?" So one of the servants of the king of Israel answered and said, "Elisha the son of Shaphat is here, who poured water on the hands of Elijah." And Jehoshaphat said, "The word of the LORD

is with him." So the king of Israel and Jehoshaphat and the king of Edom
went down to him. (2 Kings 3:11–12)

Three kings were threatened with a battle that had the potential of crush-
ing their kingdoms. They gathered their advisers, heads of state, and military
minds; yet, all of them seemed uncertain as to the outcome of the battle. They
decided to seek holy men to give them the final word—God's word for the
battle. Each of them sought out the holy men of his kingdom, only to find
inconsistencies in their predictions. Finally, the king of Judah asked a question: *"Is there no prophet of the LORD here...?"*

This was the moment when the highest title Elisha would ever receive was
bestowed on him. The answer that came forth was not a title of an earned
degree or pedigree but one of reputation. The servant of the king said, "Elisha,
the man who poured water on the hands of Elijah, is here." The three kings
called for the "water-pourer."

This behind-the-scenes prophet had actually seen twice as many miracles
as his mentor as he carried on his mantle of power; he fulfilled his double-
portion destiny. But, when it came time to look him up, they called for the
"water-pourer." He humbly accepted the title as one of high honor and dignity.
He never corrected their assumption or tried to defend his reputation as a
"real prophet." He could have told them about his double-portion miracles
or the fact that he had broken Elijah's miracle record, but he didn't, instead
accepting the title they gave to him.

It is interesting to me that all three kings were direct descendants of
Abraham. Technically, all of us are Jews from the lines of Isaac and Ishmael.
This conference of the three kings reminds me of a great day that lies ahead,
when we, too, shall stand before the Holy Trinity of God and be rewarded for
our labors on this earth. The Bible says that we will know as we are known.
(See 1 Corinthians 13:12.) It also tells us that we will receive a new name,
perhaps our true name. (See Revelation 2:17.)

In Hebrew, names have significant meanings. Perhaps our new name
will be symbolic of our life on this earth. One may be called "Soulwinner,"
another "Worshipper," and yet another "Servant." I can see the scene with
my spiritual eyes as God calls out the "Water-Pouring Club"—the Elishas

who refreshed the spirits of holy men and women. Those who step forward will be among the eternal elite, for the first shall be last, and the last shall be first. (See Matthew 19:30; Mark 10:31; Luke 13:30.) And, as Christ said to His disciples in Mark 9:35, *"If anyone desires to be first, he shall be last of all and servant of all."*

I can hear the voice from the throne as the crowns are placed on the head of each water-pourer: *"Well done, good and faithful servant; you were faithful over a few things, I will make you ruler over many things. Enter into the joy of your Lord"* (Matthew 25:21).

Twin Rivers' Elisha Ministry

At the church where I pastor, we have a ministry of elders that is truly amazing to observe. Each elder is given oversight of fifty to one hundred people, for whom they provide almost all pastoral care: they visit them, care for them, pray for them, and answer their questions about life. As you can imagine, the role of an elder is comprehensive, and it can be draining at times. In order to preserve our elders, we ask each of them to choose a personal assistant we call his "Elisha." The Elisha serves for two years, and then the elder chooses another Elisha. This ministry program has served to mentor many couples as spiritual leaders.

I will never forget when John Clark, a former Elisha, came to me one evening and asked if he could have a ceremony of blessing for the elders at the close of our monthly elders' meeting. He explained his plan, and I agreed. At the conclusion of our meeting, I invited our Elders to the sanctuary.

We walked into a setting that I will never forget. The room was lit softly, and worship music was playing in the background. There were several young men present who were either serving as an Elisha at that time or had served previously. These men had been praying for an hour, and the atmosphere of the sanctuary was filled with the sweet aroma of prayer and praise. Many of the elders began to weep as we entered the room. The Elishas arranged themselves on both sides of the aisle to bless and pray for the elders as they walked down the line.

Next, the elders sat down in the front rows as the Elishas set up a table filled with water basins and fragrant oils. As each elder approached the water basins, the Elisha who had served him poured water over his hands and spoke blessings over his life. Then the Elisha took the fragrant oil and anointed his elder's hands. There wasn't a dry eye in the house as we participated in this memorable experience.

The evening ended with all of us singing praise songs. Elder Haynes stepped forward to close the meeting by quoting the entire thirteenth chapter of 1 Corinthians from memory. The scene was electric, and no one wanted to leave. I remember looking into the tear-filled eyes of an elder and saying, "All this and heaven, too." We left that room so blessed and full of love!

DISCUSSION POINTS

1. When you think of the word "hero," who comes to mind?

2. The ministry of Father Nash was never public, but his prayers changed the lives of thousands. Discuss his testimony.

3. In what way is God speaking to your heart to pray for your leader?

4. You will see the ordinary side of the one you serve. How can you prepare your heart to serve him, even in his weakness?

5. If God calls you to be an armorbearer, He is offering you the benefits of observing the struggles, experiences, and victories in another person's life. Are you ready to answer the call?

6. In Hebrew, names have significant meanings. Perhaps your new name will be symbolic of your life on this earth. Write down some ideas of what you think your new name will be.

7. Discuss the process by which God raised up Elisha to be Elijah's armorbearer.

*"Looking carefully lest anyone fall short of the grace of God;
lest any root of bitterness springing up cause trouble,
and by this many become defiled."*
—Hebrews 12:15

5

WHO WILL BE THE ONE?

One of the saddest creatures on earth is a bitter preacher. The term is made up of two words in such violent contrast, they should never be used together. The root of bitterness is found in the original pain of disappointment, betrayal, or criticism. If we do not allow the grace we have been given to extend to those who have wounded and hurt us, we open ourselves up to bitterness. When that root begins to grow in us, many people are defiled by our bitter words, suspicions, accusations, and false assumptions.

Mighty Adversaries

What is even sadder is that many of these murmuring pastors were once mighty warriors. Now, they fight with open wounds, like blind and lame men on a brutal battlefield. Wandering from place to place, groping to find their way, they are at the mercy of anyone who will take the time to dress their wounds.

It is not easy to minister to a bitter person. Many times, these wounded warriors hold grudges from the past, fixing their minds on a source of pain that no longer exists. The more time that goes by, the more their memory gets distorted by the pain. The blood in their eyes begins to harden, and soon, their vision is impaired.

The lament of a bitter person usually goes something like this: "I used to be…" or "I could have been…" or "Look what they took from me." Many times, they blame the person who wounded them for their lack of success, when, in fact, it was their own bitterness that robbed them of joy, peace, love, and trust. They sabotaged their own success with their own attitude—by focusing on their pain. Their constant babblings produced more anguish for themselves and others. The apostle Paul cautioned young pastor Timothy about this danger, telling him to *"shun profane and idle babblings, for they will increase to more ungodliness. And their message will spread like cancer"* (2 Timothy 2:16–17).

What do we do with a wounded warrior? Do we ignore the person, or do we dress his or her wounds? There is no pat answer to this question. It is a medical question. The first thing we have to assess is whether the infection can be contained or whether it has spread and taken over other vital organs. Has it created new problems? The original wound might have been small, but now it has caused "spiritual gangrene" to set in. Is an amputation necessary to keep the infection from spreading?

While I believe it is never too late to repent or to forgive another person, we must also face the fact that we cannot undo all of the damage that has been caused. In truth, we must catch the disease of bitterness in its early stage. That is why we need armorbearers. Thousands of soldiers could have been saved if someone had been there to apply a healing balm. Too many mighty warriors have fallen unnecessarily.

The Power of One

Many warriors have been saved by the encouragement of one person. A single person can do more than you may realize. The Bible is replete with examples of what God can do with one person:

- David, a shepherd boy, turned Israel into a great nation.
- Samson single-handedly fought an entire army of Philistines.

- Paul's footprints stretched across two-and-a-half continents as he converted the Gentiles to Christianity while writing more than half of the New Testament.

- John was taken to the isle of Patmos and shown the agenda of the world for future generations.

- The woman at the well brought revival to Samaria after meeting Jesus.

God has continued to use individuals to influence society:

- Martin Luther stood against the Roman Catholic Church and hid himself away to translate the Bible into the common language because he was convinced that God's Word belonged in the hands of every individual.

- Thomas Jefferson wrote our nation's Declaration of Independence.

- Henry Ford was convinced that men could ride instead of walk, and, after three failed attempts and three bankruptcies, he created the Ford Motor Company.

- Rosa Parks got on a bus and demanded equal rights for all.

- Martin Luther King Jr. knew that all men were created equal and had the right to be free. He started a movement that would eventually break down the walls of segregation.

It takes only one person who says "I believe" and will not compromise; it takes only one person who refuses to give in to the naysayers, who stands his or her ground to be counted; it takes only one person who will walk on, press in, take a leap of faith, and see what others cannot see. If one person can save a nation or win a battle, then one person can save a church—if that one person is an armorbearer.

One Man Named David

I am fortunate to have many people in my life who look out for my well-being. I have a group of elders who constantly speak blessings over me. I have an inner circle of advisers I can talk to about anything. I have encouragers who speak into my life and people who write me letters just to lift my spirits. Unlike many preachers who serve alone, I do have close friends and even a best friend. My family and I have always lived hundreds of miles from our blood relatives, but God has richly filled our lives with people who have included us in their holiday celebrations, attended my children's concerts and other school events, and set places for us at their dinner tables. Perhaps that is one of the reasons I am now officiating at the weddings of people whom I dedicated and baptized as children. That is one of the joys of a long-term pastorate.

My family and I feel loved by our church family and fulfilled by their love and celebration of our talents and gifts. To look at our church now, it seems that pastoring it would be easy and enjoyable. And it is. I have even had other preachers say to me, "I could do what you do." I am sure they could; but doing what I do and doing what I did to get here are two different stories. For the most part, we are in a season of fruit, having come through the hardest part of "paying our dues." We are now reaping what we plowed, tilled, sowed, and cultivated. But don't be deceived by the crowds or the multimillion-dollar complex. It wasn't always this way.

I came to St. Louis to pastor a small, struggling group of people who were only months away from closing their doors. They were on a fast decline of money and people when a twenty-five-year-old pastor, his young bride, and two small babies accepted the challenge and risk of praying down a "turn-around anointing."

It was in the embryonic stage of my pastorate that God brought into my life a truck driver by the name of David. Like David in the Bible, this man never backed down from a battle. He reminded me on many occasions that I couldn't quit, because he wouldn't let me. He was the first man in my life to ever say to me, "God has given me the assigned task of making sure you complete your God-called assignment." I have to be honest—at first, I didn't know how to take his direct approach and gruff way of dealing with me. He was as respectful as a man could be, but he didn't have time to waste words and dance around issues. He quickly earned the right to call me off to the side and say, "What is going on with you? How long did you pray this week?" There were times on this journey when I viewed him as a boot camp sergeant. But I soon learned he was the one whom God had assigned to bring me back from each battle alive.

Since that time, God has sent David some help. (I must be a tough case.) But he was the first to accept the call to bring me back from the battle alive, and he holds true to that calling to this day. The most amazing thing is that I never have to tell him when I am in a battle. He always knows without my saying a word, and he always knows exactly what the battle is about. It is almost as if God gave him a secret window into my life to keep watch over my soul. I can't get anything past him. I have ceased going to him with my issues—I never have to. All I have to do is be in a room with him for five minutes, and he just knows. I can't even explain the relationship, but I do know he is the reason I made it through as many battles as I have.

I will never forget an incident that happened many years ago when David and I were on a mission trip together. We were building a church in El Salvador during the dry season there, and we ran out of water on the work site. The team was discouraged. There was no way to mix the concrete without water. Seeing the stress I was under, David came over to the crowd of people who had gathered around me and said, "Do you mean all we are worried about is water?" He lifted his head heavenward and simply asked God to send water.

It was nearing the end of the day, so we all went back to the campground where we were staying. In the middle of the night, we heard the chariots of God rolling into the camp as the clouds burst forth in rain for about thirty minutes. The national overseer of El Salvador told us that he had lived in that country for more than forty years, and that was the first time he had ever seen rain in that particular month. The rain hadn't lasted long, but when we arrived at the work site the next day, all of our water barrels were running over.

On another occasion, I saw David step in front of a swarm of hornets that he thought were going to sting me. As he stepped out, pointed his bony finger at the swarm, and spoke a word of death over them, they circled behind me and attached themselves to the wooden pulpit, where they died. They had to be scraped off of the pulpit with a putty knife. David was like a "John the Baptist" to me—always tough, never afraid of a fight; to this day, he has always had my back.

He never told that story to anyone, as far as I know, but I will never forget it as long as I live. One man can make a difference.

The Legacy of an Armorbearer

David is now in his eighties and is still just as strong in his faith as I have ever seen him. Recently, he joined me and several missionaries on a trip through the rainforests of Central America. We took canoes through the jungles to minister to the Miskito Indians.

David's son-in-law, Don, became my Sunday armorbearer. Don is a natural servant and has a heart of gold. I certainly didn't ask Don to do all the things he does, but he is determined that, on Sundays, I will be fresh when I walk to the pulpit. He meets me at the church door when I arrive and parks my car. He carries in my briefcase and anything else that I may need to take to my office. Each Sunday, he even asks me if he can shine my shoes. The spirit of David rests on the spirit of Don.

Only eternity will reveal the rewards of David's family and their legacy of preserving my family's ministry. They have saved my life more times than I can count, by refreshing me, keeping me from getting bogged down in pre-service details, making sure I get to where I need to be in the building, getting me coffee in between the services, and constantly pouring prayer and encouragement into my life.

Who Will Be the One?

There are many pulpits that would be filled with power today if there was just one person who would take on the role of armorbearer. So many pastors wear themselves out by unlocking doors, turning on lights, greeting the people as they come in the building, teaching classes, preaching sermons, praying for the sick and needy, encouraging people, counseling, visiting, handling church finances, making hospital calls, and officiating weddings and funerals. Some pastors are even expected to handle the cleaning and maintenance of the building and church grounds. Anyone can paint a wall or cut grass, but only the anointed one can cast out demons, pray the prayer of faith, and set the captives free. We don't need our men and women of God stressed out. We need their teaching and preaching in order to live in victory. We need someone who has time to walk and talk with God—someone who can walk in the anointing and take authority over sickness, depression, and oppressive spirits. What many churches are expecting is impossible to deliver. They want a shepherd, a maintenance man, and a holy man, all in one.

The most important role is that of a holy man. We need men and women of power in our pulpits. We need people whose presence, when they walk into a room, brings a sense of calm and peace. We need to free up our ministers so they can actually minister! The reason deacons were appointed in Acts 6 was to keep the ministers from waiting on tables. The word *deacon* means "table waiter." They were appointed to take care of the business of the church so that the ministers could minister. It was the appointment of deacons that caused the church to grow. The Bible says that souls were added to them daily (see Acts 16:5), but only after the deacons were in their rightful place and the ministers were freed up to do God's work. It takes only one to make the difference. Who will be the one?

DISCUSSION POINTS

1. Has your vision been impaired by bitterness or unforgiveness? Take the time *now* to pray and release those things to the Lord so that He can bring healing and peace to your heart.

2. Many mighty warriors have fallen because no one was there to apply healing balm to their wounds. Ask God to show you how to bring healing to broken and wounded people. Try to recall specific ways in which God has used you to minister to someone who was hurting.

3. Many great warriors have been preserved by the encouragement of one person. You can make a difference with an encouraging word spoken at the crisis moment of a person's life. How can you be an encourager to others?

4. It only takes one. Will you be that one? What will you do?

5. Each person should name his or her favorite Bible character and discuss how that one life made a difference.

6. How has one person changed your life?

"Let us not give up meeting together,
as some are in the habit of doing, but let us encourage one another—
and all the more as you see the Day approaching."
—Hebrews 10:25 (NIV)

6

RITES OF PASSAGE

Recently, I read a great book by Dr. Tim Elmore called *Artificial Maturity*. It primarily deals with a crisis in the generation of twenty- and thirty-year-olds who have had technology at their fingertips since they were children. As a result, they can "Google" anything and discover facts about any subject in a matter of minutes. However, many of them are lacking in life experience. And it's life experience that really brings wisdom and maturity. Knowing what needs to be done is one thing, but knowing how to do it is something else entirely. The only way to remedy this issue is by providing these young people with experiences that will reinforce the facts they look up.

Many cultures have developed rites of passage that celebrate such events as a boy's journey into manhood or when a girl grows into womanhood. These rites vary from hunting rituals to debutante balls, but the idea behind them is that children must go through a process that prepares and matures them so that they may earn the honor of being called adults.

The same must be true of spiritual maturity. Facts and stats may provide you with information, but only spiritual experiences make you mature in the Lord. An armorbearer must be more than one who simply is willing to serve or has a desire to get close to the minister. The person who fulfills this role must be _spiritually mature_. There are several rites of passage that allow one to stand with those who are mature in the faith. Without running the "spiritual gauntlet," an armorbearer could turn out to be a person of spiritual immaturity and forfeit the reward of his serving experience.

Rites of passage are tests in the literal sense. Each test measures the skill, strength, and wisdom of the candidate. I don't suggest we set up a spiritual maturity obstacle course, but I do believe God will set up His own battery of tests for each person who is called to be an armorbearer. I think the spiritual obstacle course will include such questions as:

- How do you handle opposition?
- How well do you receive and follow instructions?
- How well do you keep a confidence?
- Are you loyal, or do you talk slanderously about those you serve?
- Can you overcome pride when others don't understand why you serve?
- Can you serve when you really want to lead?
- Why are you an armorbearer? Is it because of a pursuit of prestige? Pride? Power? Calling?
- Who called you into this role, man or God?

Serving Your Way Up

Those who are called to serve in ministry will serve their way into rooms to which titles never could have granted them access. My title cannot get me into the Oval Office, but the White House maid can get in there; the photographer can get in there; even the kitchen staff can get in there. Serving will usher you into rooms, conversations, and meetings you never would have gotten into on your own.

You will meet people you would have never met otherwise. You will gain favor and influence with those whom you never would have had a chance to meet unless you had served your way into their lives.

It is true that your job will be to make the "leader of God" look good. That person will seem stronger with you at his side, helping him. But your first and foremost service must be to the Lord, not to the leader. If you set your eyes on "everything you have done for him," you will lose sight of the anointing of an armorbearer. Give service to people, but serve the Lord with gladness. My favorite passage in the Bible is Colossians 3:23–24: *"And whatever you do, do it heartily, as to the Lord and not to men, knowing that from the Lord you will receive the reward of the inheritance; for you serve the Lord Christ."*

(It may seem as though you do more for the leader than the leader does for you, but when you look back on the journey, you will see that the one you served shared the platform of his life's work with you.)What a gift that is! He provided you with experiences you needed in order to be trained up. Without him, you would have been stuck watching from the sidelines. Instead, you served your way in and obtained the keys to the most important rooms of the leader's life. You have seen the rooms of brokenness, where God trained him. You have seen the rooms of glory, where God crowned him. The armorbearer stands on duty in these rooms, secure in the gift of knowing that God used him to help bring these moments into existence. But, even in a great moment, (the armorbearer must never forget that this is a rite of passage, not a doorway of entitlement.)

The Temptations of an Armorbearer

Breaches of Confidentiality

The first area in which an armorbearer will face temptation is confidentiality. The privileged information you will have access to by virtue of your calling comes with grave responsibilities (The person you serve is not the One who called you, nor will he be the One who judges you] Like every other minister, you must answer to the One who called you—God Himself.

Entitlement

Armorbearers also must fight the spirit of entitlement. A house has many rooms, all of them serving the overall functionality of the structure. There is the dining room, where elaborate meals are served; yet there are many other rooms used for the preparations of the meal (It starts with storage rooms, such as the pantry, and the kitchen. It ends with carrying out the trash. (If you are invited into the dining room but nowhere else, it may seem as though the dining-room experience is all there is.) Only the mature know that hours of preparation and cleanup went into making the forty-minute dining-room experience a success. It is the same way in the life of a minister. Forty minutes of spiritual dining can come only from hours of preparation, cleaning, and taking out the trash.

Pride

Armorbearers also must fight the spirit of pride. Once you have seen how it's done, you may get the notion that you could do a better job. Keep in mind that God has graced you with the gift of seeing behind the scenes and allowed you to sidestep the years of trial and error, failures, and lessons learned that it took the leader to get to that moment. It takes only half an hour to preach a sermon, but it takes a lifetime to prepare for it. Books can be read in hours, but it takes living a full life of experience to write one. We are never just buying a book; we are buying a season from the author's life.

A Cup of Cold Water

He who receives you receives Me, and he who receives Me receives Him who sent Me. He who receives a prophet in the name of a prophet shall receive a prophet's reward. And he who receives a righteous man in the name of a righteous man shall receive a righteous man's reward. And whoever gives one of these little ones only a cup of cold water in the name of a disciple, assuredly, I say to you, he shall by no means lose his reward.

(Matthew 10:40–42)

This passage of Scripture seems strange when you first read it. How could we receive a prophet's reward simply by giving a cup of water away in someone's name? My father was a minister, and, when I was a boy, traveling evangelists and missionaries would often stay at our house. I certainly do not believe that I will receive an equal share of their reward in heaven for giving them cups of water, but I do believe that while they were in our house, and my mother cooked for them, she earned a share of all of the heavenly rewards they earned while under our roof. I believe that you can serve your way into the anointing of another person. This doesn't mean that you will get the reward of that person's life's work; rather, you will share in the reward of what that person is doing during the time that you take care of him.

In the same way, I believe that an armorbearer will share in the heavenly reward of the leader whom he serves, while he is serving him. Even a cup of cold water can allow you to serve your way into another's person's anointing. Therefore, developing a servant's heart is one of the key rites of passage in the life of the armorbearer. The day you start envying the badge or crown of the one you serve is the day you stop serving in his name and start serving in your own name. Maybe that is why Jesus said that in the kingdom of God, the first will be last and the last will be first. (See Matthew 20:16.)

I believe that the highest position in the kingdom of God is the title of "servant."

Jesus could have chosen the title of "King," and He would have been well within His rights to do so. Instead, He chose the title "Servant of God." And His Father has given Him a name that is above every name: "King of Kings and Lord of Lords." Serve your way up, and God will exalt you in due time.

DISCUSSION POINTS

1. Facts and stats give you information, but only spiritual experiences make you mature in the Lord. What have been some life-defining moments with the Lord that have shaped your maturity?

2. Discuss and evaluate your own "spiritual rites of passage."

3. Discuss the temptations of an armorbearer. How do you keep yourself accountable in the position that God has called you to?

4. Reread Matthew 10:40–42 and discuss. Do you have a "cup of cold water" moment you can share?

7

THE MINISTRY
OF ENCOURAGEMENT

When God created the world, He didn't make it with His hands; He spoke it into existence. He simply said, *"Let there be..."* (Genesis 1:3, 6, 14), and it was so. Many people do not realize that He put that same ability inside His children. No, we can't speak a tree or an ocean into existence like He did, but we do create the world around us with our words. The power of life and death is in the tongue (see Proverbs 18:21), and whenever we speak, we are planting either life or death in our loved ones, friends, coworkers, and acquaintances.

You Create the World Around You with Your Words

Wars have been started over words. Lives have been saved by words. Presidents are elected because of words. We should never underestimate the power of saying what we are thinking to a person whom we value. Initially, I wasn't sure if I should share any of the letters I have received through the years, but I felt it might help those in the role of armorbearer to understand the importance of encouraging their man or woman of God in this way. The letters below are only a sample of the hundreds I have received in my years of ministry, in addition to cards, e-mails, and occasional gifts.

This chapter is very personal to me. It is my way of sharing some of my choice treasures—a few of the letters that my wife, Faith, and I have received.

Dear Pastor,

I just wanted to tell you what a blessing the entire early service was to me last Sunday morning. I am sure the Scripture you shared (Matthew 11:28–30) blessed many there, but it was a direct encouragement to me.

I find that I often need to be reminded that His yoke is easy and His burden is light. I got a mental picture of a large ocean wave. I can choose to ride with that wave and have an exciting but peaceful ride, or I can choose to fight the wave, gulp water, and face possible disaster. I was reminded that I often have preconceived ideas of how God should operate in my life. Just because He isn't using me as He has always done does not mean that He is not using me, or that He is not pleased. I have been straining at the yoke and making my burden greater. I remember, very clearly, your words saying that the message does not change, yet the method may. Also, I remember that lopsided yoke illustration from your sermon years ago. Thank you for allowing the Lord to use you to remind me to get back in step!

I was so encouraged by the conversation you had with the Lord as He told you that you may not carry the gospel to the nations, but you would train those who would. Just think of how many lives you touch in doing that! This helps me to accept where I am and what He is doing with me. Thank you for being so open.

The Lord had taken me to Isaiah 58 shortly before we returned to this area. Many of the thoughts you shared confirmed to us what the Lord has directed.

We appreciate you so much. You never cease to have a current word for us all.

With much thankfulness and appreciation for you,
Mike

Dear Pastor,

I feel the Lord gave me this verse to share with you: *"You are the most excellent of men and your lips have been anointed with grace, since God has blessed you forever"* (Psalm 45:2 NIV). I am not sure why I was to share this with you, as I know how blessed and humble you feel in the way He keeps using you. Maybe it is just to be a confirmation of His love and blessings for you.

Our church family is so blessed to have you as our shepherd. I will continue to pray for you and your faithfulness.

—Edith

Dear Pastor,

I am so excited about what God is doing! I cannot thank Him enough for the changes in our lives!

We come every week to worship Him and hear a word from the Lord. It is always fresh, always new. He addresses the issues we are dealing with, or He prepares us for what is to come. He is doing so much in us and for many other people that we talk to. He is preparing His people.

God has touched many lives through the obedience of both you and Faith. It is through the worship and the washing of the Word. It is then that people are delivered from sin and set free. Freedom comes with applying God's Word.

He has proven Himself many times. We cannot stop the application. Thank you for listening to God and saying what needs to be said.

Keep looking up!

—Karen

Dear Pastor Bryan and Faith,

We wanted to tell you both how much we enjoyed the early service. The music was wonderful! The anointing was obvious and the Spirit just flowed. Faith, what a blessing it was for us! We both felt that there was a real intimacy among those who were gathered there. Thank you for giving so unconditionally of yourselves.

Pastor, I cannot tell you how I have utilized your message during my prayer time this week. Prayer is, and always has been, an important priority to me. The plan that you presented has only enhanced that time for me. I see the Lord's Prayer in a whole new perspective now, and it means even more than it did before!

Knowing that you are doing two totally different services makes it difficult for us to leave after the early service, but we realize that staying may defeat the purpose in having the two services "to spread the masses," so there is ample room for all.

Thank you both for your efforts. We pray that God will strengthen you to accomplish His purpose and give you rest, physically, emotionally, and spiritually, over the time to come. We continue to "hold up your arms" as you obediently follow His leading. How thankful we are to be under your leadership!

—Mike and Mary

I also receive "letters" in the form of artwork from children—drawings given to me at the end of the service. I have over two hundred of these drawings, and I keep them in my favorite file, labeled "Drawings from Children." Many of the children in our church bring their drawing pads to church and sketch a picture that depicts what I preach during the service. It's their way of taking notes. As I said, this file of children's artwork is one of my true treasures. From time to time, I open the file and look through the pictures again, for no other reason than that it makes me smile. Especially on rainy days or when the office is quiet, I close my door, get a cup of coffee, and sit back in my chair to peruse this file. It reminds me that what I do is important. Even though I sometimes have to wait years to see the harvest of my ministry, this file reminds me that the seed is in the ground.

The Backbone of Ministry

The ministry of encouragement is the backbone of many other ministries, yet this role often goes unrecognized. An encourager is a person who works behind the scenes and is seldom recognized publicly. I have met some of the most amazing encouragers in my lifetime. All of them poured their oil from unique vessels of uncommon love. Sherman McClenton cuts grass for free to encourage others. Pat Elam bakes pies and cakes to give away. Betty Hiles handwrites cards in the most beautiful purple ink and sends them to those she loves. I receive one every single week. Marianne Sanazaro gives hugs, smiles, and e-mails. Donna Jones sent me an e-mail every Monday for years, and now she blows me kisses from heaven. Rabon Froud would look me up after every service to tell me how good a job I had done with the sermon; now, I can't wait to look him up when I get to heaven. Vic Vierling calls our youth pastor every week just to pray with him over the phone. Bruce Hoffman checks in on me almost every week, just to make sure I'm not overstressed. You can always count on him in your "amen" corner. Mark and Stephanie Miller send songs. Billiane Cain gives the most genuine hugs you have ever experienced. Carl Whitaker always has a firm handshake and a kind word. Chris Curtis is a teenager who takes the youth pastor off to the side and prayers over him before the youth service.

Encouragers come in all colors, ages, and unique gifts. But the one thing they all have in common is that they pour into the lives of others privately, never asking for anything in return. They just give. They don't give until it hurts; they give until it feels good.

DISCUSSION POINTS

1. Share some examples of God using you to speak life into someone else's life.

2. Take time this week to ask God to highlight someone who needs to be encouraged. Then, send a letter or an e-mail to him or her.

3. How has an encourager changed your life?

4. What are the prominent character traits of an encourager?

"*You know that the rulers of the Gentiles lord it over them, and those who are great exercise authority over them. Yet it shall not be so among you; but whoever desires to become great among you, let him be your servant. And whoever desires to be first among you, let him be your slave; just as the Son of Man did not come to be served, but to serve, and to give His life a ransom for many.*"
—Matthew 20:25–28

8

ARMORBEARERS
OR ENTOURAGES?

A prizefighter enters an arena filled with cheering fans. The moment is his. Cameras are flashing, newspaper reporters are writing, and the air is charged with momentum—or, as some call it, "big mo." The hero is hidden. You catch only a glimpse of him from time to time, because he is surrounded by an *entourage*—oh yes, his people, those who keep him from the crowd by acting as a human barrier between him and those who want to touch him; those who make sure no one gets too close. They protect him by pushing people away. They escort him to the stage so that he can perform for the crowd.

This scene could accurately describe the entrance of many dignitaries, politicians, actors, performers, and athletes at their respective events. But, according to the patterns of the Bible, it should never resemble the entrance of a man or woman of God.

The Kingdom Elite

Today, the ministries of more and more pastors are starting to resemble a celebrity and his entourage. I recognize that some churches have grown so large that the crowd begins to pull and tug to the point of wearing out your emotions. Assistance and protection are necessary, in some cases, but all leaders must be careful to remember the examples set by the men of women of God in the Bible and, most important, the ministry of the Lord Jesus Himself. Every pastor of a growing church must choose integrity over celebrity. This doesn't mean that you can't have people around you, helping and even protecting you; however, the heart of integrity must always be stronger than the enticement of celebrity.

Each time the disciples started acting like Jesus' entourage, He rebuked them. We can't forget the lesson of Matthew 19:13–15:

> Then little children were brought to Him that He might put His hands on them and pray, but the disciples rebuked them. But Jesus said, "Let the little children come to Me, and do not forbid them; for of such is the kingdom of heaven." And He laid His hands on them and departed from there.

The Model of the Ministry of Jesus

Jesus had twelve men at His side. These men did much more than merely protect Him from the crowd. In Scripture, we see the disciples passing out bread and fish and then cleaning up the leftovers, among many other acts of service. They were involved in ministry along with Jesus. Who were these twelve men, and what did they do? According to their previous occupations, they ranged from fishermen and tax collectors to riotous political activists. Some were brothers, but most were strangers to each other. One thing is certain: in the world's eyes, these randomly gathered men looked like a ragtag group—a motley crew who seemed to have no hope of ever working together to accomplish anything great. Yet, this is the group Christ chose to be the first ambassadors (apostles) of the church.

The apostolic role was primarily an administrative one. Eventually, their duty would be to go from city to city, establishing order in the newly formed churches. While they were with Jesus, however, they did well to get through a meal together without an argument or debate. There was impulsive Peter, who often acted in haste. There were the "sons of thunder"—James and

John—who vied for positions of prestige. Then there was "doubting Thomas," sure to throw a damper on any dinner party. And let's not forget greedy Judas, who carried the money bag for Jesus' ministry.

In spite of the incredible odds against making anything out of this group, the Master began to pour life into them through His words. In addition, He knew that the deposit of the Holy Spirit into their lives would change everything.

In the meantime, what did these twelve men do during their three-year training program? Most of their jobs had to do with serving Christ, each other, and the crowds around them. On several occasions, we see the disciples praying for the crowd as Jesus ministered to them. Other times, they were arranging rooms for supper, fetching donkeys, and retrieving coins from the mouths of fish. They waited tables, washed feet, and even did a little cooking and grocery shopping. As participants in the ministry of Christ, they prepared the way for Him and assisted in carrying out the plan for each day. Even to the untrained eye, the role they performed resembled the role of armorbearers far more than the entourages of today's superstars.

Never Get Too Big to Serve

Those who lead must also serve, for servitude is the road to greatness. People who develop great minds but lose heart eventually become useless in kingdom work. The people of the kingdom do not do what they do because of intellectual decisions. If you merely decide to enter into kingdom work, you can decide to quit—and there will be days when you will be tempted to do just that. However, if you were called to the work, you don't have the option to quit until you first check in with the same voice that called you in the first place.

For this reason, the hearts of God's leaders must be developed along with their skills and wills. If leaders ever lose heart and get to the point of forgetting that the "kingdom elite" are servants, they have ceased to build His kingdom and have started building their own.

I believe in giving honor where honor is due. I believe in serving holy men and women. But I also believe the ones being served should never grow too comfortable as the recipients of service. It is easy to get to the point of expecting or even demanding service before ministry is "performed." That should never be the case. Yet, in the midst of the thronging multitudes, it's easy for someone to feel so exalted that he or she begins to lose sight of what the Lord saw in him or her to begin with.

Never Forget Your "Journey" to Greatness

We must never forget where we were when Jesus picked us up. We must never forget our moments of desperation, when our assignment was bigger than our skill. We must never forget our days of loneliness, when He took us to the wilderness, a place without distractions, in order to teach us important lessons. We must never forget the small beginnings; the people who invested in us early, the encouragers who believed in us when we didn't believe in ourselves, and the people who mentored and recognized gifts of greatness in us when we couldn't even see how to get through the week. We can't allow the pressing crowd to fool us into thinking that they are the ones who made us important enough to be celebrated. The crowd loves what we give them, but the armorbearer loves us even in our struggles.

It was on the journey that God trained us, taught us, and built our character. It was in the backfield that God chose David to be king. Jesus chose His disciples when many of them were either "down and out" or still wallowing in their sin. He chooses the foolish things of the world to confound the wise for a reason. (See 1 Corinthians 1:27.) God wants the ordinary to become the extraordinary in order to further display His glory. But we must never forget how the Lord's Prayer ends: *"For thine is the kingdom, and the power, and the glory, for ever"* (Matthew 6:13 kjv).

It is always His kingdom, His power, and His glory—regardless of our success. Our journey is the insurance, so that when we rise to the top, we remember to give Him the glory for all of it. Without struggles, we might begin to get the impression that it was our gifts and talents alone that caused us to rise. The struggle keeps us humble and dependent on God.

Servers or Strutters?

We must never get arrogant in our anointing, for *"pride goes before destruction, and a haughty spirit before a fall"* (Proverbs 16:18). We need to realize that even great men and women get tempted. Even the giants in the kingdom, the mighty men and women of God, have a thorn in the flesh that buffets them, just as the apostle Paul did. (See 2 Corinthians 12:7.) We are not above struggles or moments of weakness; therefore, we cannot turn our armorbearers into entourages. They must remain the warriors at our side, faithful servants who help us fight the real battles—not strutters who "sashay" with us through the crowd and parade us around, making us look important.

The key to kingdom leadership is servitude, regardless of your status; you will never attain a level at which serving becomes optional. Perhaps the greatest reason the disciples served instead of strutted is because of what took place behind the scenes in the ministry of Christ. Fortunately for us, the Bible records some of the most intimate moments Christ spent with His disciples. For example, in John 13, we read about a very personal moment Christ had with them just before His crucifixion. In this scene, He leaves them with a powerful example of how to be a leader in the kingdom of God.

> So when He had washed their feet, taken His garments, and sat down again, He said to them, "Do you know what I have done to you? You call Me Teacher and Lord, and you say well, for so I am. If I then, your Lord and Teacher, have washed your feet, you also ought to wash one another's feet. For I have given you an example, that you should do as I have done to you. Most assuredly, I say to you, a servant is not greater than his master; nor is he who is sent greater than he who sent him."   (John 13:12–16)

There are so many other things Christ could have done or said to leave a lasting impression on these twelve men He had chosen to lead His church, but nothing could have had more impact than the act of girding Himself with a towel and washing their feet. Peter was so humbled by the gesture that he tried to refuse it, at first. I would have loved to witness the reactions of these men as the Lord showed them His servant's heart.

If we truly believe that leadership begins at the top, then leaders who are being served must ask themselves if they are also washing the feet of those who lift their load. The bottom line is this: Do you have the mentality of an armorbearer or an entourage? (Leaders who are servants will most likely be surrounded by armorbearers. Leaders who are more into being served than serving others have an entourage.)

Saying Please and Thank You

As children, we are taught to always say "please" and "thank you." That childhood lesson should be a point of reference for those of us being served by armorbearers. As leaders, we should never make the mistake of thinking that the "God-called" are "on call" for us 24/7. We are not the masters of those who serve us; rather, we are partners with them in ministry. It is just as important for us to recognize their gifts as it is for them to recognize our gifts. Armorbearers are not anointed to wash our cars or do our yard work for us. If they choose to give this gift as a way to encourage or to free up our time and energy, they may offer to do so, but tasks such as these should never be expected. Armorbearers have been anointed for prayer, spiritual warfare, and encouragement. If everyone being served remembers the simple courtesy of saying "please" and "thank you," it will serve as a constant reminder that it is a privilege to serve, but it is even more humbling to *be* served.

> The challenge of leadership is to be strong, but not rude;
> be kind, but not weak;
> be bold, but not bully;
> be thoughtful, but not lazy;
> be humble, but not timid;
> be proud, but not arrogant;
> have humor, but without folly.

—Jim Rohn

DISCUSSION POINTS

1. Jesus poured His life into the lives of His disciples, despite their weaknesses. Who has God placed in your path so that you can pour into him or her?

2. Do you have a favorite disciple? If so, explain why.

3. Jesus had intimate moments with His disciples, teaching them how to be servants. Discuss a time when God spoke to you and asked you to serve someone.

4. Discuss this phrase: "We must choose integrity over celebrity."

5. Discuss the section on the importance of saying "please" and "thank you."

"*Then all the trees said to the bramble, 'You come and reign over us!'
And the bramble said to the trees, 'If in truth you anoint me as king over
you, then come and take shelter in my shade; but if not, let fire come out
of the bramble and devour the cedars of Lebanon!'*"
—Judges 9:14–15

9

DISCERNING THE HEART
OF THE MOMENT

The call of the armorbearer is to assist the leader, but it is important to allow the leader to lead. When two people attempt to lead at the same time, it's a lot like two men carrying a heavy couch—if you don't decide who is leading, you'll end up dropping it.

I Can Tell by the Look on Your Face

Ministry involves its share of intense moments, and simply reading the facial expressions of a leader may cause you to overreact to a situation that is already under control. Before and after worship services are prime opportunities to misread facial expressions and subsequently misjudge a leader's true intent.

As a pastor, I sometimes get into what I refer to as "the zone." For me, "the zone" is the hour before I am scheduled to speak; it can also be a period of time spent retooling a few of my message points before speaking again. It is quite easy to view "the zone" as a time when I am unsure, troubled, or worried; but, in reality, I am just thinking deeply and processing my thoughts. An armorbearer who misreads these moments may try to step in and intervene, attempting to protect the leader from a problem or threat that doesn't exist. In times such as this, it is best to wait for the leader to make a request— to verbally express his concerns—before you act.

In the event that a security matter is brought to the attention of an armorbearer, he must be able to discern whether it is worth troubling the leader over. To do this, he must gather adequate information on the issue, because it's the right information that gives you the confidence to make the right decision. Insufficient information weakens you and makes you vulnerable to harmful situations. As a leader, I prefer to know when there is a troubling situation, even if the knowledge messes with my head a bit. But it's usually the armorbearer, along with church security, who must make the call and determine whether something is a legitimate matter of concern or just a harmless soul who wants attention. Communication between the armorbearer and the leader is absolutely necessary. Good communication will foster trust and confidence, while poor communication, or the lack thereof, breeds insecurity and creates an atmosphere of distrust.

Praying with Your Armorbearer

I have always been intrigued by the story of God taking the Spirit that rested upon Moses and laying it upon the elders of Israel.

So Moses went out and told the people the words of the LORD, and he gathered the seventy men of the elders of the people and placed them around the tabernacle. Then the LORD came down in the cloud, and spoke to him, and took of the Spirit that was upon him, and placed the same upon the seventy elders; and it happened, when the Spirit rested upon them, that they prophesied, although they never did so again. (Numbers 11:24–25)

Other Bible accounts describe the same process of impartation, such as when the mantle of Elijah came to rest upon Elisha, or when the disciples sent forth new ministers into ministry with the laying on of hands. I believe that an armorbearer should pray regularly with the leader he serves, so that their hearts may be knit together by the Spirit of God. It is important that the two people operate as one, spiritually. Yes, one will lead, and the other will follow, but the follower must know the heart and footsteps of the leader. Prayer is the best method I know for maintaining a spirit of unity. If an armorbearer fails to pray with the leader he serves, then he forfeits his unique calling and becomes just another member of the hospitality ministry or the security team. But when an armorbearer prays with his leader, the two of them can become another Moses and Joshua, Elijah and Elisha, or Paul and Timothy.

Getting Through the Crowd

I love the people I serve, so I don't need to be protected from them. It is a joy for me to have a few moments of connection with them before and after a worship service. My armorbearer and I always go into the sanctuary about ten to fifteen minutes before the service, just so that I may walk through the crowd, giving hugs, prayers, and encouragement. I love to show up in the balcony, where they least expect me and seldom get to see me up close. When I show up there, they always seem to be excited, surprised, or confused. It's just fun!

After I finish speaking at our earliest Sunday service, I attend a breakfast welcoming new people to our church. I don't get to eat; I just go in and meet everyone in the room. We call it the Pastor's Breakfast. It's really a "meet the pastor" breakfast. It is always difficult for me to get from the platform to the meet and greet. I am sensitive to the crowd, and I never want to be rude to them, so I depend on my armorbearer to get me through the crowd without going into "tackle" mode.

Occasionally, I may get "trapped" by a person who wants to chat, even though there is a line of people behind him or her. Some people want to receive instant personal counseling right after the service. Others want to tell me about their favorite "God moment." For the most part, this is never a problem. On occasion, however, the captive must be set free! It is important to have discussions with your armorbearer so that you both are on the same page about how to handle those moments of "captivity." Otherwise, the loyal armorbearer might deal insensitively with a very sincere person who is full of zeal but has no wisdom in the moment. There are easy ways to get out of these situations, but you have to be able to recognize the signals so that everyone knows the plays.

Guts and Glory

I believe that those who serve as armorbearers have a special call from God on their lives. When Moses was on the mountaintop with God, the only one who got to see the glory was his armorbearer, Joshua. Elisha was the only person to feel the whirlwind that took Elijah the prophet. God's leaders will experience glorious moments in their lives, and their armorbearers will certainly share in those experiences.

Glorious moments are not without responsibility. Many times, they are accompanied by loads to bear—mental burdens and heavy spirits. When an armorbearer senses that his leader is under such a load, he must avoid the inclination to coach his leader in the name of encouragement. A football coach may tell a quarterback, "Get back in the game!" or "Hold your head up high!" Unlike others who serve in the church and see on the sunny days in the leader's life, the armorbearer will see him when he bleeds. And when an armorbearer sees his leader in a moment of insecurity or weakness, his goal should not be to get his leader back in the game as quickly as possible. God often uses brokenness to bring strength into our lives, and the armorbearer must be patient while his leader gains strength through difficult circumstances.

DISCUSSION POINTS

1. Have you ever misread someone's facial expressions? What was the result?

2. When we withhold vital information from someone, we may actually put them in harm's way, even if our intentions are good. If we are trying to protect someone, it is extrememly important to know when, where, and how to deliver pertinent information that affects their security and/or the security of others. Discuss some hypothetical situations in which this truth applies.

3. Communication is crucial when we are trying to follow a leader. Both the leader and the armorbearer have responsibility to communicate. Do you agree that information brings confidence, while a lack of information brings insecurity? Why or why not?

4. Try to come up with some clever ways to move a leader through the crowd without sending the signal that the leader does not care about the people.

"When the Philistines were at war again with Israel, David and his servants with him went down and fought against the Philistines; and David grew faint. Then Ishbi-Benob, who was one of the sons of the giant, the weight of whose bronze spear was three hundred shekels, who was bearing a new sword, thought he could kill David. But Abishai the son of Zeruiah came to his aid, and struck the Philistine and killed him. Then the men of David swore to him, saying, 'You shall go out no more with us to battle, lest you quench the lamp of Israel.'"
—2 Samuel 21:15–17

10

KEEPERS OF THE FLAME

David was a giant-killer. (See 1 Samuel 17.) As a matter of fact, this confrontation was the very gift God used to bring him into his kingship. Can you imagine hearing the people singing songs about the exploits of David? "David has killed his tens of thousands," they sang. Children would run to meet him in the streets, chanting songs of praise after his victories. In a matter of days, this no-name son of Jesse became a household name and Israel's hero.

But, even for the heroes of the world, life moves in seasons. Many a hero has experienced the reality that importance and recognition are fleeting. That which is relevant and effective in one season of life may not be so in a later season. As a matter of fact, one of the most difficult things for a leader to discern is when to let go of something that once made him great.

The Battle of the Giants

The expectations of the crowd can sometimes push or pull you away from God's will for a new season and a new harvest of blessings. The fact that David killed giants, fought battles, led armies, and walked in courage led Israel to love and accept him as their king. He overthrew the Jebusite stronghold and moved his kingdom to "Jebus-salem" (Jerusalem), the ancient city of King Melchizedek. He conquered lands far and wide for his people. All David had to do in order to boost national morale was to take his army to war and return home with the spoils. The victory parades were endless. The people danced in the streets, feasted for days, and experienced prosperity throughout the land. On many occasions, David even gave gifts to everyone at the festival. Who would have wanted to miss one of King David's parties? The only thing he had to do was keep winning battles.

But, while Israel was dancing in the streets, season after season, their young king was aging. With each new campaign, it became more difficult to live up to his notable reputation. The giant-killing, street-dancing, race-running hero was aging. Finally, the day arrived when David could no longer fight battles with the strength of his youth. In his younger days, he said, *"By You I can run against a troop; by my God I can leap over a wall"* (2 Samuel 22:30). But the passing of years had changed some of that. In his heart, he could still do all of those things; but, in reality, his body would not allow him to leap over walls anymore.

During one particular battle, David came up against one of the sons of the giant. The title alone indicates that the large man was much younger than David. However, in typical Davidic fashion, he arrayed himself in warring garments and showed up with the boys. This particular Philistine had one aim in mind: he wanted to be known as the one who killed the giant-killer. His sole purpose that day was to kill David. His name was Ishbi-Benob, and he was sporting a new sword and spear as he waited for the perfect time to make his move.

When the moment arrived, Ishbi-Benob stood face-to-face and toe-to-toe with the man who had built his reputation by killing his relatives. When Ishbi-Benob lunged at the slower-moving king, his blow knocked David to the ground. The older man seemed to be no match for the young, confident giant. Ishbi-Benob stood over the king, ready to strike a death blow that would change both of their reputations. That's when Abishai, one of Israel's war champions who happened to be nearby, saw that David was faint and came to his aid. The king had worn down his opponent, but it was Abishai who had to finish the job. As the day ended, the men of David gathered around their king and said, in effect, "This is the last time you go to battle with us. We have to keep you alive, or else the lamp of Israel will go out!" (See 2 Samuel 21:17.) The younger men were saying, "We can do what you used to do. Right now, we need you to lead us. Let *us* fight the battles while *you* lead and train us with your wisdom and years of experience."

A Man Reaps What He Sows

Let him who is taught the word share in all good things with him who teaches. Do not be deceived, God is not mocked; for whatever a man sows, that he will also reap. For he who sows to his flesh will of the flesh reap corruption, but he who sows to the Spirit will of the Spirit reap everlasting life. And let us not grow weary while doing good, for in due season we shall reap if we do not lose heart. Therefore, as we have opportunity, let us do good to all, especially to those who are of the household of faith.

(Galatians 6:6–10)

The apostle Paul, who never minced words, wrote a straightforward command to the Galatians. Yet this passage is seldom understood or preached in the intended context. Pay close attention to the language of the text: *"Let him who is taught the word share in all good things with him who teaches."*

Paul is figuratively saying that it is wrong for a person to receive instruction, teaching, and guidance from a teacher without giving back something in return. It is wrong to gain from a man or woman's knowledge, resources, and life experiences and not give anything back.

I have never understood how a person can endure pain almost to the point of death, emerge victorious, write it down in a book, and then face complaints from people about having to pay a few dollars for the book. If a person spends years on the battlefield and learns how to defeat the enemy, it is well worth a few dollars to learn those strategies instead of going into life blindly and learning them firsthand. Too many warriors are wearing out because they are giving more than they are receiving. They are like empty wells that brought life to so many weary travelers, yet no one took the time to pour back into them.

Paul says those who receive instruction should *"share in all good things."* He is speaking, in particular, about the good things that come through the teaching one receives.

This means that if a teacher gives you the principles to walk out of defeat and into prosperity, then, when you come into your blessing, you should remember his house. If you don't, you are in the wrong. You have, in fact, taken a man's resources, applied his knowledge, become successful, and left him to hurt alone.

It is easy to become empty when everybody is taking from your gift and none of them is giving back from the blessings received. It leaves you feeling used up, taken advantage of, and lonely. Most ministers do not expect anything in return because they willfully and gladly serve God with their gifts. That is even more reason to bless them. Too many of them come to the end of their days because they can no longer *"run against a troop"* or *"leap over a wall."* They are discarded or demoted instead of being sought to teach others what they have learned.

God Is Not Mocked

It is in this very context that we hear the words *"God is not mocked; for whatever a man sows, that he will also reap"* (Galatians 6:7). In other words, it is not just an injustice to the teacher; it also is a mockery to God. The Lord is saying, in effect, "I take the time to raise up leaders, call them out, and train them, and all I want you to do is take care of them so they can give you what it took Me years to develop in them."

God chooses men and women and places angels around them to teach them. Angels lead these warriors through dark places, rough battles, and the school of hard knocks. Others, God sends to the classrooms of seminaries, where they often have to trust Him for every payment just to finish their education. Many are guided to foreign soil in order to gain what they need to become effective ministers. God wrestles with them to deliver them from their pasts, their sins, and their shortcomings. He orders their steps to take them down paths where few have gone and highways from which many have never returned.

At the end of this journey of development, God presents our teachers as gifts to His body. He says, "Now, learn from your leaders. I have prepared them and gifted them with a special heart, a unique calling, and a wealth of experiences so they may be a guiding light in your life. Take care of these men and women so they will not become weary in their work."

God expects us to pour back into our teachers to enable them to continue guiding and instructing us and others. If we take and do not give, eventually, we will be the ones who lose. If you read on in Galatians 6, you will get to verse 9: *"And let us not grow weary while doing good, for in due season we shall reap if we do not lose heart."* Why should these ministers grow weary while doing good? The answer is because no one is pouring back into their lives. They keep giving and giving, while no one takes notice of their needs or pains. Too many great teachers have lost heart. Too many have become weary and quit. Too many have given up while doing a good thing.

It is a mockery to take a person's resources without showing gratitude. God says that if you don't understand this principle, you will reap a harvest of corruption in your own life; if you take and do not give, it is selfish, and selfishness is sin of the flesh. He says that if you then try to sow what you have received selfishly, you will be sowing to the flesh. In turn, you will reap a whirlwind of flesh as your harvest.

God is saying that it is wrong for you to go home with hope in your heart while your teachers go home and cry themselves to sleep. It is wrong for you to learn from a teacher how to turn your finances around and then do nothing to help when that teacher struggles to make ends meet. It is wrong for you to receive help that saves your marriage while the teacher struggles in his own marriage because no one has taken notice of his weariness. It is wrong for you to grow in the Word while the teacher tires from lack of rest or proper vacations or sabbaticals. It is wrong for you to be healed emotionally while the teacher is discouraged and depressed because everybody takes and no one gives back.

Just Pour a Little Water Before You Leave

This true story is an apt illustration. There was a well that was dug in the middle of the desert. A small hut was built over the well so that any weary traveler who was thirsting to death could find it and live. It was miles away from the nearest source of water. Only desperate people arrived at this desolate place. When a traveler found the hut, there was a jug of water by the hand pump with a note on it that said, "If you pour the water from the jug into the pump, this deep well will give you all the water you need, but you must pour the water from the jug in first to prime the pump. When you leave, be sure and fill the jug up again, or the next traveler will not be able to get any water from the well."

Each desperate person had to make a decision whether to drink the water in the jug or take the risk of pouring it down the old hand pump in order to prime it. Each time someone poured the water out by faith, he did so knowing that if the old well was dry, he would die of thirst in the desert. But the fact that the jug still had water in it gave him hope that someone else had traveled that way before and left water in the jug. Once the water was poured into the pump by faith, the thirsty traveler would then desperately start pumping the handle, and, soon, as much water as he could drink would come gushing out. He'd have enough water to wash, fill his canteen, and drink his fill. But he had to be responsible enough to remember to fill the jug before leaving so that the next traveler could get to the water. If only one person neglected to fill the jug, the water would be inaccessible from that time on.

Many teachers are like that old well. All they need is a little in order to give a lot. We have to remember that when our lives have been saved by the water that was filled with hope and instructions, we need to take time to fill the jug before we leave. If we do not give back, soon, another weary traveler will come to that same well, but the pump will be dry. There will be nothing wrong with the water—it will still be there—but there will be no way to get to it because the pump has dried out.

Keepers of the Flame

Their duty included the ark, the table, the lampstand, the altars, the utensils of the sanctuary with which they ministered, the screen, and all the work relating to them. And Eleazar the son of Aaron the priest was to be

chief over the leaders of the Levites, with oversight of those who kept charge
of the sanctuary. (Numbers 3:31–32)

Go with me in your imagination to the tabernacle of Moses, erected in the wilderness wanderings of Israel. I want to walk you through a typical day for the Levites. Their job was to keep the tabernacle and the ordinances of God operating at all times. Each Levite priest had specific instructions. Some gathered wood and carried it to the altar. Some tended to the water in the laver. Some baked and changed out the bread in the Holy Place. Others washed the priestly garments.

Many of them were assigned to sing, play musical instruments, and fill the atmosphere with praise. One of the Levitical duties was to make sure the light of the candlestick never went out. It had to burn continuously day and night. It was the symbol of Christ and the Holy Spirit in the tabernacle. In order to fulfill this responsibility, they had to keep fresh oil and wicks nearby at all times.

A few years ago, I preached a series of sermons entitled "The Tabernacle of Moses." I broke down each symbol and piece of furniture to its primary function, as well as its symbolic meaning. When I got to the candlestick, it was easy to see that it was a symbol of Christ. The candlestick was made in appearance like an almond tree. Its branches had knobs, buds, and flowers on each stem, modeled after an almond branch in the spring of the year.

The Hebrew word for *almond* means "awakening," which is an allusion to the almond blossom, the first to bloom in the spring. The almond's pinkish-white blossoms always appear before its leaves. The awakening of Jeremiah's ministry started with an almond branch. (See Jeremiah 1:11–12.) The rod of Aaron that budded was an almond branch; Jeremiah's and Zechariah's *"Branch of righteousness"* (Jeremiah 23:5) was an almond branch. The trunk of the candlestick (or lampstand) symbolized the *"Branch of righteousness"* (the Messiah) and the first to bloom in the spring, which spoke of Jesus and the resurrection.

The lampstand had six other branches. In prophetic Scripture, *six* is the number of man. This, too, speaks of us being engrafted into the true Vine, which is Christ. (See John 15:1.) The bowls at the tops of the candlesticks were shaped like almonds. They symbolized the fruit of the tree, or the fruit of the Spirit (see Galatians 5:22–23), as it relates to the life of the believer.

There is an interesting principle that must not be overlooked in this spiritual analogy. The fire comes out of the fruit; the fruit cannot come out of the fire. The anointing of God comes through lives that bear fruit, not gifts. Over and over again, God said to His people, "*Be fruitful and multiply*" (Genesis 1:22, 28; 8:17; 9:1, 7; 35:11). We must never rely solely on our gifts to bring God's anointing. It is the fruit of our lives He desires.

The fire and the oil in the bowls represent the work of the Holy Spirit. But the fire can burn only if it has a wick. The wick had to be trimmed daily by the priests, according to Exodus 27:21. It is that daily trimming that catches my attention. This majestic golden candlestick, with its pristine, pure oil and its brilliant flame, depends on a tiny wick in order to give its light. The brilliance of the room is lost if the wick is not trimmed.

The radiance of this Holy Place is never seen if the wick is not trimmed. The table of bread is never discovered. This tiny, free-floating wick, while barely noticed because of the flame, is absolutely key to keeping the Holy Place alive and lit. This wick, among virgin oil and pure gold, is the only element of imperfection in this entire scene, yet it is an absolute necessity. The wick is the natural conduit needed to get the oil and flame to the room. The wick can wear out, wear down, and even burn out. That is why it is necessary to trim it every day so that the lamp will not go out.

This wick is the minister. It is the imperfect path by which God transfers the supernatural into the atmosphere of the natural. It is the small, vulnerable conduit of transferred anointing. This tiny, oil-soaked piece of straw and cotton allows the oil to get to the flame, and the flame to get to the darkness.

We need men and women who will take it upon themselves to be keepers of the flame. Oh, that God would raise up wick-trimmers, oil-pourers, and fire-lighters, so that the wicks God has chosen to be His spiritual conduits will keep the flame burning!

DISCUSSION POINTS

1. How do you discern when to let go of something that once made you great?

2. Second Samuel 21:17 says, in effect, "We can do what you used to do. Right now, we need you to lead us. Let us fight the battles; you lead and train us with your wisdom and years of experience." Discuss.

3. In Galatians 6, Paul said that it is wrong for a person to receive instruction, teaching, and guidance from the life of a teacher without giving back to the teacher in return. What have you learned from the life of a teacher, and how can you give back to him or her?

4. The anointing of God comes through lives that bear fruit, not gifts. Discuss the fruit of the Spirit and how to walk in them daily.

"Now Amalek came and fought with Israel in Rephidim. And Moses said to Joshua, 'Choose us some men and go out, fight with Amalek. Tomorrow I will stand on the top of the hill with the rod of God in my hand.' So Joshua did as Moses said to him, and fought with Amalek. And Moses, Aaron, and Hur went up to the top of the hill. And so it was, when Moses held up his hand, that Israel prevailed; and when he let down his hand, Amalek prevailed. But Moses' hands became heavy; so they took a stone and put it under him, and he sat on it. And Aaron and Hur supported his hands, one on one side, and the other on the other side; and his hands were steady until the going down of the sun. So Joshua defeated Amalek and his people with the edge of the sword."

—Exodus 17:8–13

11

HANDS ON, HANDS UP, AND HANDS UNDER

Going Before the People

One of the most difficult tasks for a leader is to let go. When a ministry is born, the leader is with the people, fishing rod in hand, as a "fisher of men." (See Matthew 4:19; Mark 1:17.) In fact, in the early days of a ministry, it is usually the leader who is leading people to the Lord, discipling them, caring for them, training them, and giving them their first kingdom assignments.

At this stage, the leader's fellowship and friendships are within the congregation. The leader is everyone's "buddy," and together, a community of faith and friendship is built. This "with the people" relationship can be rewarding, but, like all intimate relationships in which other people know your business, it can also be painful.

One of the tragedies of leadership is when the leader becomes overprotective of the things God asks him or her to manage. God is always the landlord of kingdom property. When you assume ownership of an area that is not rightfully hours, it becomes difficult to release people into their own ministry or into another field of labor into which God has called them. "With the people" ministry, while socially rewarding, is also limited, for it is possible to maintain fruitful friendship with only a certain number of people at a time.

In the Old Testament, in order for spiritual growth to occur in the lives of the leadership and the people alike, God had to send Moses and the elders of Israel "before the people":

> And the LORD said to Moses, "Go on before the people, and take with you some of the elders of Israel. Also take in your hand your rod with which you struck the river, and go." (Exodus 17:5)

The people were complaining and murmuring against Moses. They had become too familiar with him and the other leaders. Familiarity often breeds contempt. But when God moved Moses and the elders beyond the people, they were able to separate themselves from the common concerns and focus on the bigger picture. Not only that, but now they were also able to fellowship more closely with God and hear His voice more clearly.

This began to produce miracles in the midst of Israel, because this new level of leadership came with a new level of anointing. Water flowed from a rock, and everyone's thirst was quenched. It is almost impossible to lead when you are walking with the crowd. You can't lead from the middle of the pack; you can lead only when you're out in front. If you want to know if you are leading, look behind you to see if anyone is following you. If you have a following, you are a leader; if not, you are only taking a walk. Going "before the people" released Moses from the day-to-day cares of life and the murmurings of the people. With a clear mind and heart, he was able to speak the words of the Lord to the people.

Going Above the People

The leadership ability of one man or woman alone will not cause a church to grow. Effective leadership is the ability to raise up many leaders within the congregation. When this occurs, it's only a matter of time before the leadership capacity of the organization will grow to the point where the leader must separate once again in order to take the church to the next level. It is in the "high places" with God that you will find the greatest anointing of your ministry. This is the third dimension of leadership.

Level one is "with the people."

Level two is going "before the people."

Level three is when God calls you "above the people."

"Above the people" does not refer to social status. It does not mean that you are better than the people; it means that God is establishing order within the congregation, and He is calling you to a spiritual high place so that you may better lead your diverse and growing group. Because of this, there is a crucial issue that faces the leader whom God calls to "go up": loneliness. At this level, you may be feeling out of control because you are no longer directly in touch with the lives of the people you lead.

One of the things Moses had to do was send down someone he trusted to fight "with the people." His only option was to use someone whose trust had been with him through all three levels. He chose Joshua, whose loyalty was unquestioned. He needed someone who didn't require his help in order to solve every problem. Moses knew that Joshua could fight without burdening him with all the details. At his new level, Moses did not need to solve problems of that type any longer. He needed someone who could handle the battle without Moses' having to hold his hand.

Hands On and Hands Up

Joshua needed to be "hands-on" with the ministry in order for Moses to have his "hands up." You cannot have your hands up and be "hands-on" at the same time. You will never be able to climb to the spiritual levels required of you unless you can let go of the hands-on experience.

Hands-on ministries are intimate and socially fulfilling, but they are limited. The higher you climb in levels of ministry, the more you have to separate yourself from the people you are serving. In Jesus' ministry, He started out teaching thousands. Eventually, however, He chose twelve to lead and three to accompany Him to the higher spiritual places.

As you begin to go higher, your only companions are those whom you trust with your life. Trouble will come to your leadership system if you move someone from level one to level two or three when he is not ready. Not everyone proceeds upward at the same rate. Not everyone can be in the inner circle. When you bring someone into your inner circle who does not have your back, you are asking for trouble.

Some people need to remain in the outer circle. Those in the outer circle may love you for your gift, but they don't really know you. Those in the middle circle may serve you, but they will turn on you as soon as you offend them. Those who go up with you are the people who serve and stay with you, no matter what.

Elijah gave Elisha several opportunities to leave, but he never did so. He earned the right to be in the inner circle because of his commitment to the prophet.

You can go higher only when you find people who will place their hands under your tired arms. The highest place of church leadership is the place where spiritual warfare is fought and won. It is the place where you tear down strongholds and kill spiritual giants. It is a rare dimension that few ever reach.

The leader who goes up enters that realm with a dilemma. First, the people you serve want your gift, but they do not always want you. Second, your middle-management level of leadership wants to be with you all the time because that is the way they have grown accustomed to operating. They are still before the people, where they need to be, but now, you have gone to a higher level and separated from them. They miss you, and you miss them. But, in order for you to help them go free, you must move into the higher realm and go toe-to-toe with the principalities and rulers of darkness. When you enter the third dimension of leadership, you go there with a heavier spiritual load, and with the smallest support system you have operated with in years.

Hands Under

The inner circle of Moses' life was entrusted to his older brother, Aaron, and his brother-in-law, Hur. The historian Josephus says that Hur was the husband of Moses' sister, Miriam. These were the two people Moses trusted the most.

Joshua knew how to fight "with the people." He was the "hands-on" leader. The elders of Israel knew how to lead "before the people." They became the "hands-up" leaders. Remember that Moses took them to the mountain of God to meet with Him.

The group had become firmly established with spiritual leadership: the operational side, run by Joshua, and the spiritual side, run by Aaron and the elders. With this leadership structure in position, it was time to defeat and conquer their enemies.

The battle took place in a valley—symbolic of the places we live, but more so of the places we fight. The army gathered and Joshua prepared to fight.

Of course, there is only so much a human army can do, for *"our struggle is not against flesh and blood, but against the rulers, against the authorities, against the powers of this dark world and against the spiritual forces of evil in the heavenly realms"* (Ephesians 6:12). As the army marched into battle, the elders remained behind the lines, with the women and children. I am sure they were interceding in prayer and giving comfort and assurance to those whose family members were going into battle.

Moses took his position atop the mountain, carrying his rod—a tangible symbol of divine power that God had given him. It was the same rod that had consumed the sorcery of Pharaoh's wizards, called down plagues onto Egypt, parted the waters at the Red Sea, and brought miracles in the wilderness.

He had his rod and his position with God, but that was not enough. The long battle was tiring. As long as Moses' hands were up, Israel prevailed, but when he grew weary and his arms dropped, the enemy began to win the battle. His two most trusted confidants—the members of his inner circle—saw what was going on and rushed to his side. As a great leader, you can't let just anyone see your vulnerabilities. You can be transparent but not weak. Transparent communication allows people to relate to you, but those same people should not be aware of your most personal struggles.

These two men who loved and trusted Moses held up his arms during the battle. In the end, the battle with the Amalekites was won, but not because of Joshua. As good as he was, they would have been defeated that day if the outcome had depended only on his abilities. It was not even won because of Moses. Moses was great, and his rod was with him, but his flesh was too weak for such a long battle. The battle against the Amalekites was won that day because of Aaron and Hur. Without them being in place to hold up the weary hands of this great leader, the battle would have been lost.

"Hands-on" will get you only as far as the first level of leadership and victory. "Hands up" will take you higher and will set the people free. But the only way to put the enemy to flight and take charge of the spiritual atmosphere within your sphere of assignment is to have "hands-under" ministers in place who will be there to make sure that you do not quit too early, that you don't wear out too quickly, and that you don't become weary in well-doing.

Thank God for armorbearers!

DISCUSSION POINTS

1. If you want to know if you are leading, look behind you to see if anyone is following you. Can you identify any people who are following your lead? Are your family members, friends, church members, and children following you?

2. How can you clear the path for your leader to allow him to lead from the front?

3. Discuss how you can protect your pastor from gossip and negativity as he goes to the next level of leading people and fellowshipping with God.

4. Discuss the characters of Aaron and Hur. What type of men do you think they were? Why did they go up with Moses instead of someone else?

5. Discuss the inner circle of a leader's life. How many people do you think such a circle should comprise? What are the qualifications of the members of this group?

"When the Son of Man comes in His glory, and all the holy angels with Him, then He will sit on the throne of His glory. All the nations will be gathered before Him, and He will separate them one from another, as a shepherd divides his sheep from the goats. And He will set the sheep on His right hand, but the goats on the left. Then the King will say to those on His right hand, 'Come, you blessed of My Father, inherit the kingdom prepared for you from the foundation of the world: for I was hungry and you gave Me food; I was thirsty and you gave Me drink; I was a stranger and you took Me in; I was naked and you clothed Me; I was sick and you visited Me; I was in prison and you came to Me.' Then the righteous will answer Him, saying, 'Lord, when did we see You hungry and feed You, or thirsty and give You drink? When did we see You a stranger and take You in, or naked and clothe You? Or when did we see You sick, or in prison, and come to You?' And the King will answer and say to them, 'Assuredly, I say to you, inasmuch as you did it to one of the least of these My brethren, you did it to Me.'"
—Matthew 25:31–40

12

PORTRAITS OF
ARMORBEARERS

In the U.S. military, chaplains are not allowed to carry a weapon. Instead, when on the battlefield or in dangerous situation, each chaplain is assigned a bodyguard.

I want you to imagine a scene: there is smoke all around you, and the sounds of war are deafening—the cries of the wounded, the whistling of missiles in the air, the buzz of bullets flying around you. It's overwhelming, to say the least. All you can think about is finishing the mission and going home. Each warrior is armed and dangerous. Each has a weapon or piece of artillery designed to engage the enemy and protect his or her own life.

Yet, in this place of bravery, there is a group that stands tall in their private and world of unsung heroism. These elite warriors are known as military chaplains. They are on the same battlefield, but their only weapon is faith. Many of them are injured or killed while serving men and women who are ready and desperate to call on the name of God in their hour of danger. They baptize converts in the trenches and hold services in tents or in the open air. They serve sacraments, give counsel, carry the wounded, and comfort the dying with a Bible in their hand as their only weapon they need. This brave lot can be found wherever there are soldiers. Chaplains are on ships, aboard planes, and in the trenches with the fighting forces. They answer the call of every national and international crisis, be it a war or a disaster relief team.

One of the reasons they can be so brave is because each of them is assigned an armorbearer. That is not their official title, but it is an accurate description of their assignment. The job of these armorbearers is to go into the combat zone with the chaplains and protect their lives while they minister. The armorbearers stand in front of the chaplains and lead them to places of safety. They stand behind the chaplains while they lean over dying soldiers who are within minutes of death. They cover chaplains while they carry the wounded to a place of safety. While others are fighting the enemy, these lone soldiers are protecting the chaplains with their own lives.

The duality of this team is what makes it work. Chaplains would not be able to perform their duties without the aid of the brave armorbearers who watch their backs. This amazing portrait of protection gives a vivid real-life picture of one who protects another so that he may give his best. Many of these brave ones will receive a medal of honor in this lifetime. But in the other realm of reality, the heavenly realm, another reward awaits them—a crown of glory that does not fade away.

Windtalkers

In World War II, nations of the world came together as allies to stop German and Japanese aggression. Advances in technology made this war the first one to feature air strikes and heavy artillery. It seemed as though the sides were well matched. The onslaught of killing and devastation continued to claim lives in a series of bloody battles.

War is always ugly, and this one was no different. One of the problems encountered by U.S. armed forces was the fact that the enemy kept breaking their radio codes, making it impossible to communicate on the battle field to turn the tide of the war. They needed a new resource, and they found it in the heart of the Native American Navajo nation.

The Navajo had been repressed by white settlers for many years. They had been driven off their lands and stripped of both pride and resources. However, when the horrors of war reached American soil, the Navajo decided to put aside their grievances and pull together in order to protect their homeland.

The Navajo had a gift that was needed in this battle—a complicated language made up of voice inflections that, when slightly altered, changed the entire meaning of the word or phrase. Even today, the Navajo language is considered one of the most difficult to master in the world. To the uninitiated ear, Navajo communication sounds more like a series of grunts and moans.

The U.S. military employed the Navajo to send instructions and locator messages for military commanders in the field. If the enemy intercepted these messages, they were not able to translate them. The Navajo native tongue was better than any code that had been devised. The enemy was baffled, and the tide of war turned to our favor, all because of these brave Navajo "windtalkers."

Since the war depended on radio operators to send and receive the orders or give the position of the enemy, the safety of each Navajo was of utmost importance. Each Navajo soldier was given a personal bodyguard to keep him alive in battle. The bravery of these bodyguards—these armorbearers—was just as important as the bravery of the windtalkers. Each man had to fulfill his role in order to help win the battle.

Many battles turned because of this new communication tool. However, the messages never could have been delivered without the fearlessness of the people who kept the windtalkers alive. They pulled them from foxhole to foxhole, and several of these armorbearers even sacrificed their own lives for the sake of the cause. Many of these men had to lay aside their own preconceived prejudices in order to serve honorably.

The example of the windtalkers and their armorbearers is an incredible picture of people who lay aside their personal agendas to serve a greater cause.

Military Medics

It seems as though armorbearers do their best work in places where others do not want to serve. They don't always serve in dangerous places, but they serve people whose presence is vital to the success of a plan, purpose, or organization.

In this chapter, we have dealt primarily with wartime scenarios. I like these portraits because they depict people who are willing to put their lives on the line to serve another. While these illustrations may seem extreme, they are real-life situations that show the character and bravery of those who serve.

Another example of bravery exemplified in the gravest of situations is exemplified by military medics. They risk their own lives in each enemy engagement. The troops in combat are in the business of taking the lives of the enemy, but the medics work tirelessly to save the lives of the troops.

They work under dirty, bloody, smoky, and dangerous conditions, performing surgeries in an instant, in order to bring others home from war. Without regard for their own safety, they go wherever the danger is, because that is precisely where their patients are to be found. Many of them have lost their own lives in an attempt to save the lives of others.

These conditions are unique because they portray a lifesaver working to protect another lifesaver. This reminds me of the story in Nehemiah 4, in which one group of men worked to build a protective wall around Jerusalem, while another group protected them from the enemy with spears and bows. The work of the craftsmen hinged on the ability of the armorbearers to protect them while they labored.

When the Going Gets Tough, the Tough Get Going

The walls of heaven are surely lined with the trophies and medals awaiting these selfless servants. Their secret sacrifices have not gone unrecorded in the courts of heaven. I am certain that celestial beings sing their heroic anthems. "By and by, when the morning comes, and all the saints have gathered home," I believe we will hear songs written by angels to commemorate and declare the eternal glory and honor of those who served silently and selflessly.

Perhaps this is why the Lord said that the first will be last, and the last will be first. (See Matthew 19:30; Mark 10:31.) If heaven has parades, I believe it will be the armorbearers who will wave from the streets as people line the sidewalks and grandstands to celebrate their lives.

Never let it be said that armorbearers can't do anything but serve. On the contrary, they are the toughest of the tough. They are the bravest of the brave. Their servanthood comes at great cost. They must overcome jealousy, pride, and selfishness to take up their crosses and follow Christ. This elite group knows nothing but private victory, for the honor tends to go to the ones they serve.

Their coronation still awaits them. I can't wait to see their crowns, to discover their new names, and, most of all, to hear our Lord say, *"Well done, good and faithful servant....Enter into the joy of your lord"* (Matthew 25:21).

DISCUSSION POINTS

1. Armorbearers go into war with their leader. The Bible says that God will make your hands as a skillful warrior. Have you allowed God to train you for war? Have you joined your pastor in the fight for your city?

2. Laying aside your personal agenda to serve a bigger cause is the life of an armorbearer. What is God calling you to sacrifice for the sake of the big picture?

3. Discuss the heavenly rewards that await every faithful armorbearer. What types of honors do you think will be given to this elite group of servants?

4. What are the character traits of an ideal armorbearer?

5. Discuss the types of leaders in the kingdom of God who need armorbearers.

THE ARMORBEARER'S PLEDGE

I Am an Armorbearer...

◆

I will stand in the face of adversity, for I have been anointed to bring God's leader back from battle.

◆

I will overcome temptations of negative conversation, for I fight at the back of the one whom God has assigned to me for preservation.

◆

I will not feel sorry for myself when my efforts go unnoticed, because my reward will come at the end of the battle, when the King crowns me with eternal honor.

◆

I will stand in the whole armor of God and make sure my leader does not wear out.

◆

I will pray, for prayer is how I dress my leader with the armor of God for the day.

✦

I will check on the wellbeing of my leader, for God has entrusted him or her to my care.

✦

I will encourage my leader for I am a keeper of the flame.

✦

I can and will fulfill this divine assignment because I am confident in my calling, secure in my position, anointed in my service, and prepared for the challenge!

✦

I am prayed up, fired up, and, every day, I will sharpen up, until the day I go up to meet the One who filled me up and called me up.

✦

I am not afraid of ridicule, nor ashamed of giving my glory to another, for, one day, I will stand before my Commanding Officer, Jesus, the King, to receive my rewards for service.

✦

I will fight a good fight, finish the course, and keep the faith, for I am am one of God's armorbearers.

ABOUT THE AUTHOR

Bryan Cutshall and his wife, Faith, have been in ministry together since college, where they first met. Bryan is the senior pastor of Twin Rivers Worship Center, a multigenerational, multisite church in St. Louis, Missouri. Under his leadership, Twin Rivers has grown from 52 people to become one of the most vital megachurches in the Midwest. Bryan is also the founder of Church Trainer. Each year, he trains thousands of pastors and leaders in the U.S. and abroad to be on the cutting edge of church leadership by staying fresh, relevant, and passionate about what they do.

Bryan is also a church consultant who has done extensive research and training in the area of church growth, with a particular emphasis on lay ministry development. He trains thousands of church leaders every year at conferences, diagnostic clinics, consultations, and retreats.

He is the author of several books, in addition to the Church Trainer book label—a resource line for training pastors, leaders, and workers in the body of Christ. All of his books and resources can be found at www.churchtrainer.com.

His other titles published by Whitaker House are *Your Promised Land Awaits* and *Unlocking the Prophecy Code*.